THE FIRST
EMPEROR
OF CHINA

By the same author

Confucius: A Biography

Pirate King: Coxinga and the Fall of the Ming Dynasty (published in paperback as *Coxinga and the Fall of the Ming Dynasty*)

The Moon in the Pines

A Brief History of the Vikings

The Dorama Encyclopedia: A Guide to Japanese Television Drama since 1953 (with Motoko Tamamuro)

The Anime Encyclopedia: A Guide to Japanese Animation since 1917 (with Helen McCarthy)

The Little Book of Chinese Proverbs

THE FIRST
EMPEROR
OF CHINA

JONATHAN CLEMENTS

SUTTON PUBLISHING

First published in the United Kingdom in 2006 by
Sutton Publishing Limited · Phoenix Mill
Thrupp · Stroud · Gloucestershire · GL5 2BU

British Library Cataloguing in Publication Data
A catalogue record for this book is available from the British Library.

ISBN 0-7509-3959-1

Typeset in 11/14.5pt Sabon.
Typesetting and origination by
Sutton Publishing Limited.
Printed and bound in England by
J.H. Haynes & Co. Ltd, Sparkford.

In memory of
Roger Zelazny
1937–95

We are all shadows

Contents

List of Illustrations and Maps

Preface and Acknowledgements

Demonised for centuries, the First Emperor is an imposing figure, even in classical accounts. Our chief written source for him is the *Record of the Historian*, a vast chronicle of ancient China by the Han dynasty author Sima Qian that includes biographies of many of the major figures of the era. But the First Emperor is also a shadow. In his own lifetime he was often aloof and hidden from view, protected by distance from killers and admirers alike. None dared look at him or speak his true name, so it is unsurprising that we have little idea of his facial features or character. There is not much in ancient accounts about his personality other than the bold architectural statements and the brutal political decisions. A biography of the First Emperor is, by necessity, also a biography of those closest to him – of the past works, more than 40 per cent of Cotterell's *First Emperor of China* is devoted to the politics and history of the Warring States, while the protagonist of Bodde's *China's First Unifier* is not the emperor at all, but his wily chief minister, Li Si. As for original sources, we have decrees issued in the name of the First Emperor, but little of his personality, although the *Record of the Historian* includes biographies of his ministers, his generals and even the man who tried to kill him. The First Emperor himself is that silence in between, the subject they dare not mention or the distant sovereign in whose name they claim to act.

There are inferences that we can draw from certain asides and moments – the conqueror of China is also the man who ran from an assassin, tugging in vain at an unwieldy ceremonial sword that was too big to draw from its scabbard. He was the man who had everything and yet was plagued by signs of his own mortality. He was the ruthlessly secular thinker, defying the old gods and yet still trying to join their number. Despite his hatred and censure of superstition, we now know that his burial featured divine gestures of faith and power rivalled only by the pyramids of Egypt. For 2,200 years before the discovery year of 1974, nobody guessed the First Emperor's final monument, designed to last forever but presumed destroyed within years of his death, lay beneath the red clays of Lintong.

It was Jaqueline Mitchell at Sutton Publishing who first suggested a book on the Great Wall, and who then allowed me to talk her round instead to a book about the man who built it. My agent, Chelsey Fox of Fox and Howard, ensured there was blood for the drums. My former history tutor, Ellis Tinios, thought he had retired from the University of Leeds, only to find himself standing on his desk late one Saturday evening, a phone jammed in the crook of his neck while he squinted among his papers for a Xiongnu chronology. Andrew Deacon was similarly surprised to find me pestering him for chemical analyses of Chinese cement; Motoko Tamamuro was prevailed upon to translate obscure legends; and Frederik L. Schodt and Fiametta Hsu dutifully trudged through a Central Asian desert with a camera without once offering a word of complaint. Anthony Barbieri-Low of Pittsburgh University and Cary Liu and Nicole Gordon of Princeton University Art Museum combined their efforts to get me a precious rubbing of an ancient wall carving depicting the events of my prologue. Payment in dollars was resolved through the kind assistance of Adam Newell and Kimberly Guerre. The librarians of London's School of Oriental and African Studies were their usual unflappable selves. And finally, thanks to Kati, who provided a peaceful kitchen table on which I could park my laptop, and who gained her black belt while this book was being written. Had the Red Prince been able to hire her, history would have been different.

My grateful acknowledgement goes to Stanford University Press for permission to quote from *Xunzi*, translated by John Knoblock, and *The Annals of Lü Buwei*, translated by John Knoblock and Jeffrey Riegel; to the University of Michigan's Center for Chinese Studies for permission to quote from the *Chan-kuo Ts'e*, translated by James Crump; to Indiana University Press for permission to quote from volumes I and VII of *The Grand Scribe's Records*, translated by William Nienhauser *et al.*; and to E.J. Brill for permission to quote from *China's First Unifier* by Derk Bodde.

Chronology

by a Yan general.

283 Birth of Anguo. Xunzi arrives in Chu.

280 Li Si born in Qi. Birth of Han Fei.

278 A Qin general captures the Chu capital and burns the ancestral tombs.

276 Revolt in Chu.

265 Death of Queen Dowager Xuan.

c. 261 While being held hostage in the state of Zhao, minor Qin princeling Yiren befriends merchant Lü Buwei.

c. 259 Lü Buwei lets Yiren have his concubine, Zhaoji, who some claim is already pregnant.

258 Zhaoji gives birth to Zhao Zheng, later Ying Zheng, who is presumed to be the son of Yiren.

257 Qin engineers bridge the Yellow River by lashing together boats. Siege of Handan. The servant Zhao Sheng dies to save Yiren, who henceforth feels obliged to care for his son Zhao Gao. Presumed commencement of studies of Li Si and Han Fei under Xunzi.

256 Qin troops dethrone the Son of Heaven, ending the Zhou dynasty.

251 Death of the Bright King. Enthronement of Anguo as the Learned King. Ying Zheng returns to Xianyang, the Qin capital, with his parents. Sudden death of the Learned King.

250 Yiren is enthroned as the Merciful King. Lü Buwei is made grand councillor. Work presumed to begin on the *Annals of Lü Buwei*. Xunzi leaves Qin.

249 Lü (homeland of Confucius) conquered by Chu.

248 Birth of Liu Bang (future Han Emperor).

247 Death of the Merciful King. Li Si decides to leave his master Xunzi and seek his fortune in Qin.

246 The thirteen-year-old Ying Zheng is the new king of Qin, with his 'Second Father' Lü Buwei acting as regent alongside his mother Zhaoji. Li Si becomes a senior scribe.

244 Famine, a plague of locusts and outbreaks of disease threaten the security of Qin. Lü Buwei offers ennoblement for a fee paid in grain.

c. 239 Work is completed on Lü Buwei's ultimate encyclopaedia, *The Annals*. Death of the Lady of Summer. Sighting of Halley's Comet. Death of Chengjiao.

238 Rebellion of Lao Ai. Assassination of Lord Chunsen, prime minister of Chu. Xunzi loses his post in Chu. Ying Zheng undergoes his ceremony of manhood.

237 Lü Buwei exiled to Sichuan. Li Si becomes minister of justice. Another comet. Attempt to exile all foreigners from Qin.

235 Lü Buwei commits suicide.

234 Qin armies attack Zhao and Han.

233 Han Fei, famous philosopher and former classmate of Li Si, meets an untimely death in Xianyang. Li Si's mission to the state of Han.

232 The Red Prince returns to Yan without the king of Qin's permission.

231 Presumed commencement date of the Red Prince's assassination plot.

230 Qin conquers Han. Completion of the Zheng Canal project. Death of the Lady of Glorious Sun.

228 Qin conquers Zhao. Death of Zhaoji.

227 Jing Ke's assassination attempt on Ying Zheng, masterminded by the Red Prince.

226 Qin army storm the capital of Yan, forcing the Red Prince's father to flee north-east to Liaodong.

225 Qin conquers Wei. Qin armies advance on Chu.

224 Centenary of the accession of the first king of Qin.

223 Qin conquers Chu.

222 The last of the Yan defenders is defeated in Liaodong; official date of the fall of Yan.

221 Qin annexes Qi, the last remaining state. The ruler of Qin now controls the entire region understood to constitute 'the world'. Distant barbarians eventually refer to it by the name of its conqueror, as 'China'. In celebration of the imposition of one rule over the entire region, Ying Zheng assumes the new title – First Emperor. First reference to the construction

of a tomb at Mount Li. Division of the former seven kingdoms into thirty-six imperial prefectures. Possible date of Gao Jianli's assassination attempt.

220 Imperial inspection of the Great Wall zone north of the Qin heartland.

219 The First Emperor tours his domain, intending to make sacrifices at Mount Tai and sending out the first of several missions in search of the elixir of life. Li Si becomes grand councillor.

218 Imperial entourage heads east again. Assassination attempt masterminded by Zhang Liang; discovery of the conspiracy of the Ji family.

217 The year in which 'nothing happened'. The First Emperor dabbles in Taoist mysticism and possibly makes undercover expeditions to observe his subjects.

216 While walking alongside a canal in Xianyang, the disguised First Emperor is assaulted by local criminals.

215 Second quest for the elixir of life. The First Emperor is warned of the danger presented by *Hu*.

214 A new campaign conquers provinces in south China, known as *Nanhai*, the South Seas.

213 The Burning of the Books. First cometary observation for twenty years (presumed to be interpolated by the later Han dynasty).

212 Massacre of 460 scholars. Banishment of Prince Fusu. Construction under way on the Afang palace.

211 Discovery of a meteorite inscribed with a prophecy of the First Emperor's downfall. Mars, the 'Executioner of Heaven', does not leave the constellation of the Heart.

210 Death of the First Emperor. Death of Xunzi.

208 Zhao Gao takes over. Execution of Li Si. Tomb-builder Zhang Han turns his labour gang into a fighting force to repel invaders.

207 Zhao Gao presents a deer to the Second Emperor. Zhang Han pursues Qin's enemies across the border, but eventually defects in fear of his life.

206 Death of the Second Emperor. Crowning of Ziying as 'king', not emperor. Ziying submits to the rebels and is executed. Xianyang is destroyed and the tomb of the First Emperor is reportedly desecrated (although this may refer to the tomb complex and not his actual grave).

202 After a civil war, Liu Bang is proclaimed as the first of the emperors of the new Han dynasty.

200 The Han capital, Chang'an, is established across the Wei River from the ruins of Xianyang.

195 Liu Bang orders twenty households to move to the site of the First Emperor's tomb to guard it from souvenir hunters.

AD

1932 In Lintong, a local farmer finds a terracotta head.

c. 1940 Mount Li is fortified, leading to the discovery of several artefacts during the digging of trenches.

1961 The First Emperor's tomb is designated a national historical site.

1973 Discovery of many complete ancient manuscripts preserved as silk scrolls in a grave in Mawangdui.

1974 Peasants find the terracotta army while sinking a shaft for a well.

1975 Discovery of Judge Xi's grave in Hebei.

1976 Archaeologists uncover the first of several construction sites that were homes and workplaces to the original tomb-builders.

1978 Archaeologists uncover pits of sacrificial animals and rare birds near graves presumed to be of the First Emperor's executed sons.

1981 Discovery of high quantities of mercury at the main mound; possibly the remains of the 'mercury sea' thought to have once surrounded the coffin.

1987 The First Emperor's tomb is designated a World Heritage site by UNESCO.

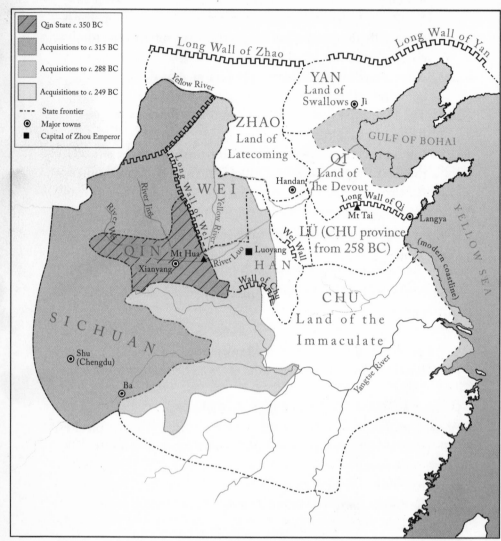

The Expansion of Qin.

PROLOGUE

The Dagger in the Map

Confucius said: 'Those who do not think ahead will find their troubles close at hand.'[1] It did not take a wise man to see that Ying Zheng wanted to rule the entire world. His ancestors had begun the slow progress of conquest. His grandfather, the Bright King of Qin, had deposed the Son of Heaven himself, leaving the world nominally rulerless. Now, Ying Zheng was thirty-three years old, presiding over a nation that struck fear into the hearts of its neighbours. His country was a machine of war, a state run on military lines, its citizenry regimented and harshly disciplined. Such an environment created a people bred for conquest, and the state of Qin was steadily eating up its rival nations.

Something needed to be done. In Yan, the Land of Swallows, the Red Prince decided he would not wait for the warlike Qin peoples to march over his borders. The army of Qin was infamously ruthless; for the Red Prince himself, there would be no quarter, for he had once been a friend of Ying Zheng, and a noble hostage who had escaped from the kingdom. When Qin attacked Yan, the Red Prince was going to die. The Red Prince thought ahead and hatched a plot of assassination.

The planning was elaborate. There was no way a killer could sneak past the walls, guard posts and bodyguards that surrounded the king of Qin. In order to get close enough, an assassin would have to gain the trust of the king and his ministers. The Red Prince needed someone who would undertake the mission, a deed that would result in certain death, for even if the killer somehow made it through the many defences and struck a fatal blow, his chances of getting out alive were slim. The assassin would need to be supernaturally lucky, or perhaps stupendously sure of himself.[2]

1

The Red Prince found his man. His name was Jing Ke. He was, he claimed, an expert swordsman, one who had trouble selling his services to noble clients. Perhaps his attitude was to blame; he famously got into fights with other swordsmen over the subject of sword-fighting itself. Perhaps he was never as proficient as he boasted; once, an argument over a chess game in the town of Handan turned violent, but Jing Ke fled before he could prove himself in combat with his opponent, Lu Goujian. This was, however, one of the incidents that brought him to the attention of the Red Prince's advisers, who saw in Jing Ke not cowardice, but an ability to keep a cool head in tense situations. While Jing Ke's swordsmanship had never been put to the test, he had found other ways of making a name for himself. He associated with the wrong crowd, and was often found drunk in the marketplace in the company of a dog-butcher and a musician.

He seemed like an unlikely candidate to save a nation, but he came on the highest recommendation. In order to preserve the utmost levels of secrecy, the Red Prince's chief adviser took his own life after suggesting Jing Ke, both to conceal the plot and convince Jing Ke of its importance. Armed with the news of the adviser's suicide, the Red Prince begged Jing Ke to take the mission. The nature of the deal they eventually struck is unclear, but Jing Ke agreed.

Faced with the prospect of making a one-way trip, Jing Ke took his time.[3] A voluntarily condemned man, he undertook lavish last meals, indulged in luxuries fit for a king, and dallied with a succession of slave girls supplied for his pleasure. Later legends, considered too frivolous for inclusion in the *Record of the Historian*, have Jing Ke skimming golden coins across a pond, feasting on the liver of a priceless horse, and even maiming a pretty musician so that her hands might be presented to him on a jade platter.[4]

Whatever the actual nature of his debauchery, Jing Ke took his sweet time. The Red Prince grew concerned about his choice, wondering if the assassin would ever begin the mission. And while Jing Ke enjoyed his many, many last requests, the Qin war machine rolled ever onwards, conquering the Land of Latecoming, where the Red Prince had once lived.

As Jing Ke continued to enjoy himself with his luxuries and his bedmates, the Red Prince looked for the means to carry out the deadly mission. Realising that, in the unlikely event of Jing Ke reaching the king's inner chamber, he might only have seconds to carry out his task, the Red Prince searched for the ideal weapon. No sword, axe or spear would get past the king's protectors, but a small dagger might. The Red Prince's aides, unaware of the purpose of their quest, were sent out in search of the sharpest in the world. Eventually, they found something that seemed to fit the description: a knife in the possession of a refugee from the Qin conquest. He was persuaded to part with it for a hundred measures of gold and sent on his way, ignorant of the purpose to which it would be put.

The Red Prince also experimented with poison. Its speed of action was not really the issue; more important for a diligent assassin was the required effective dosage. The king might be armoured; he might be struggling. When the assassin struck, he might only have the opportunity to make the slightest of cuts in his quarry's skin. The Red Prince's experiments cost many lives – slaves struck with poisoned blades until the assassin was convinced he had found the concoction that could deliver death from the smallest cut. As the Qin army drew ever nearer to the border, the Red Prince felt obliged to mention that time was running out.

However, Jing Ke was still not ready for his mission. He reminded his client that it would still be necessary somehow to get close to the king of Qin, and that this would not become suddenly easy. He would need a ruse to gain the king's confidence, some way of making it past the outer guards, a means of evading the chamber sentries and the personal bodyguards. The king of Qin was notoriously, understandably, paranoid and unlikely to let a stranger near his royal person unless that stranger had somehow done a great service to his kingdom.

Jing Ke had an idea. He had heard that Fan Yuchi, once a loyal general of the king of Qin, had fled his former master and sought sanctuary with the Red Prince. There was a high price on his head – a thousand measures of gold (almost half a metric tonne), and a noble rank, the rulership of an area comprising ten thousand households. Jing Ke asked for his head.

The Red Prince was scandalised. The general had come to him for help, and he could hardly have him killed merely to satisfy his own scheming desires, whether it meant the plan would fail or not. The Red Prince was adamant; he would not order the death of the refugee general Fan Yuchi. Accordingly, Jing Ke himself went to see Fan Yuchi. The former general brooded alone somewhere on the Red Prince's estate, his entire family already dead at the hands of the king of Qin. Jing Ke told him that he had heard of the massive reward on the general's head and asked him what he planned on doing with his life.

The general had no answer. His family was dead, and no career with the military of his former enemy awaited him; the men of Yan would never follow him in battle. He told Jing Ke the truth, that he could do nothing but sit in exile and dream of revenge.

In one of history's strangest business proposals, Jing Ke offered a deal. He asked for Fan Yuchi's head. In return, he promised to avenge him by taking his head to the king of Qin to claim the reward. When the grateful king admitted Jing Ke into his presence, Jing Ke planned to grab him by the sleeve and pull him close, stabbing him with the poisoned knife.

'Day and night,' replied Fan Yuchi, 'I gnash my teeth and eat out my heart trying to think of some plan. Now you have shown me the way!'[5]

The *Record of the Historian*, the ancient Chinese book from which this story comes, implies that Fan Yuchi acted immediately, but it is more likely that he thought about it for some time, before seeing that Jing Ke's harsh plan was the only way he stood a chance of avenging himself. He cut his own throat.

The Red Prince received the news with some shock. He dashed to the general's chambers and found the body sprawled where it had fallen, its blood in a trail across the floor. He embraced the general's corpse and wept 'in deep sorrow', the *Record of the Historian* claims. We can only speculate about the Red Prince's true emotions – relief perhaps that the brave general had taken the terrible decision out of his own hands; hope that his last, desperate scheme now had some chance of success; despair that with each step of the plan, he was forced to become ever more ruthless and calculating, turning him into a copy of the enemy he despised, the king of Qin.

The Red Prince ordered the head of Fan Yuchi to be cut off and placed inside a box. Now it would be possible for Jing Ke to feign loyalty by presenting the king of Qin with the head of his enemy. Yet Jing Ke still did not leave.

He could not arrive in Qin alone; that would still look suspicious. The Red Prince found a local man, Qin Wuyang, a fierce criminal who had committed his first murder aged just thirteen. Wuyang was capable of great violence, a berserk fighter who could spring into action at the slightest provocation. The Red Prince thought he would be ideal as a travelling companion for Jing Ke – an unobtrusive youth who could keep the king's courtiers occupied when the crucial moment came. There is no mention in the *Record of the Historian* of what price Wuyang demanded for his services.

When Jing Ke still did not leave on his mission, the Red Prince lost his patience, suggesting that perhaps Wuyang might be able to accomplish the mission on his own.

The *Record of the Historian* records a cryptic response from Jing Ke. With great reluctance, he agreed to leave, remonstrating with the Red Prince that Wuyang did not stand a chance on his own, 'setting off with a single dagger to face the immeasurable might of Qin'.[6] Jing Ke also explained that the reason he had delayed so long was that he was waiting for a friend. In his opinion, the mission required three assassins, not two, and he had sent word to the ideal candidate to complete the team. The *Record of the Historian* does not reveal the identity of this mysterious third man, but later events and asides suggest that it was Lu Goujian, the chess-playing swordsman from whom Jing Ke had once fled.[7]

Whoever and wherever he was, he had taken too long to arrive. Time was running out for the state of Yan, and the Red Prince considered his end of the bargain fulfilled. It was time for Jing Ke to set out.

It was a history-making expedition. If it worked, Qin would be plunged into chaos, and its neighbours could shake themselves free. They might continue to fight among themselves, but it would at least end the tyranny of Qin. The Red Prince would live on. So many brave men had died already to make the mission possible: the adviser who committed suicide to preserve the secret; the unwitting slaves who had tested the poison; and the noble general Fan Yuchi, who had provided Jing Ke with his vital bait. The chronicles are silent about the many others who may not have made it into the history books – it is unlikely indeed that any of the servants or concubines in Jing Ke's mansion were permitted to live past the day he left.

The Red Prince handed Jing Ke a rolled-up map revealing details of Yan's most important strategic sites. To an enemy who wanted to invade, it would be more valuable than any general's head. It was one more bargaining piece to get Jing Ke into the presence of the king, and if it failed, Yan's defences would be wide open.

For a mission of such weight, carrying the destructive power to throw one kingdom into chaos or cause the full-scale ruin of another, the departure of Jing Ke and Qin Wuyang was necessarily low key.

The two assassins were accompanied to the Yan border by the handful of nobles who knew their secret. Clad in the white robes and hats of a funeral procession, both as cover and in acknowledgement of the mission's one-way nature, the group picked their way along the border road. It was a chilly, blustery day, and the procession stopped at the river that marked the edge of Yan territory. There, the Red Prince conducted a sorrowful sacrificial rite to the god of travel. Jing Ke's friend, the musician Gao Jianli, played a mournful tune on his dulcimer, and Jing Ke sung of the cold winds, the freezing river and the doomed existence of brave men.

Then, even as the attendant nobles blinked back tears, Gao Jianli shifted key, striking up a brisk, military tune in a new register, designed to spur soldiers on the march. Even as the men present stood up straighter and glared across the river at the domain of their enemy, Jing Ke sung the same words again, but this time in defiance, anger, and with a sense of purpose:

> The winds howl around us
> The river runs cold
> As the valiant depart
> Never to return.[8]

6

As the tune finished, Jing Ke and Wuyang climbed into their carriage and set off, their wheels rolling out of the mud of the river bank and onto a new track. Without a backward glance, they left Yan behind and journeyed into a land that had been conquered by their sworn enemy, the hated king of Qin.

It was a long journey to Qin itself. The two assassins had to traverse many hundreds of miles of conquered territory, and alongside the Royal Domain, where once the ruler of the known world had resided, but now in ruins after the Qin conquest. Eventually, their carriage entered the state of Qin itself, the forbidding land under a permanent state of martial law, from whence the Qin armies had fanned out across the known world. On the banks of the Wei River, they reached the king's capital.

There, they approached one of the king's leading courtiers, presenting him with rich gifts. They then tried their most cunning ruse of all, hiding in plain sight by announcing directly to the courtier that they were on a secret mission. We have no way of knowing with what suspicion the Qin government or its spies may have regarded the journey of these two arrivals, but their announcement ensured that if any of their clandestine behaviour had been witnessed during the long journey, they now had a ready alibi.

The assassins told the courtier that their mission had been kept secret because of its vital diplomatic importance. They claimed to be envoys from the king of Yan, sent to arrange a peaceful solution to any potential hostilities between their nations. If the king of Qin objected to the Red Prince's harbouring of the fugitive general Fan Yuchi, then he need not concern himself any more, they said. Nor had the government of Yan taken a weasely diplomatic solution and simply bundled the general out of their territory to another state or the barbaric wilderness; this had, in fact, been the original suggestion of the Red Prince's advisers when the general had arrived. No, boasted the assassins, when the people of Yan said they sought an alliance with Qin, they meant it, and as proof they had brought with them the general's head.

There was more. The ruler of Yan, so claimed the assassins, was not content merely with handing over the remains of the fallen general. He was afraid, they said, literally shaking at the thought that the king of Qin might find some other reason to go to war with Yan, as he had done with so many other luckless kingdoms. The ruler of Yan wanted no part of such conflicts. He was ready to concede defeat before battle had even been joined, indeed, before war had even been declared. He knew that the king of Qin coveted a borderland region of strategic importance, but there was no need for their nations to come to blows about it. Here, said the assassins, was a detailed map of the region in question; the Red Prince's father, the ruler of Yan, was ready to hand it over immediately to his ally, the state of Qin.

Had the ruler of Yan been present, such concessions would have been news to him, as would the assassins' claim that he was ready to acknowledge the king of Qin as the overlord of Yan itself. But the assassins kept up the pretence, even to the extent of humbly asking that the ruler of Yan be permitted to continue tending the altars of his ancestors. Such a request was completely in keeping with tradition – the ruler of Yan would thereby continue sacrificing to his forefathers, thereby ensuring that none of them were tempted to avenge themselves on the conquering king of Qin from the afterlife.

It was a tall tale, but stranger things had happened during the reign of the king of Qin. Although the policy-makers of the Qin government placed little value on the sayings of Confucius, had not the sage of olden times once said that a truly enlightened ruler should be able to sit in his palace and do little, as the wondrousness of his government attracted new followers?

As was the tradition of messengers in ancient China, Jing Ke's words were regarded as those of the ruler of Yan himself. When Jing Ke bowed in humble supplication, he did so supposedly as a proxy of the Red Prince's royal father, claiming that the ruler of Yan had himself bowed in his own courtyard as he sent his messengers on their way.

The chief minister was convinced and conveyed the news to the king.

Ying Zheng, the king of Qin, was an imposing figure who had already sat on the throne for more than half his life. An enemy once described him as having a waspish nose, elongated eyes, the voice of a jackal and the heart of a tiger or a wolf.[9] He had survived palace intrigues and attempted revolts, and believed himself already cursed by the restless spirits of the nations he had conquered. He controlled much of the known world from his palace in Xianyang, but if he feared anything at all, it was the retribution that might be visited upon him by the spirit world.

But there was, it seemed, good news from the Land of Swallows. Instead of needing to plan for yet another military expedition, the king now had evidence that his conquest was nearly done. The king joyfully donned his richly decorated robes, girding himself with a ceremonial sword, and called not only for his assistants, but their assistants and their assistants' assistants, so that nine ranks of courtiers, hundreds of men in all, assembled to witness the great moment – a kingdom conquered without the need for a battle.

The two 'envoys' from the Land of Swallows walked into the palace past armoured guards with swords and savage 'dagger-axe' halberds. Jing Ke raised the box containing the general's head so that all in the room might see him. Behind him, Wuyang carried the heavy roll of the map, concealing the all-important dagger within it. They walked along an aisle in the king's great hall, through the crowd of assembled ministers. The king they had come to kill waited for them at the other end, sitting alone on a raised dais.

Although the advisers of the king despised the traditions of Confucius, there were still some policies that they readily adopted. One was the political application of *feng shui* – an acknowledgement that the character of a state could be conveyed through architecture. Government buildings were designed to instil respect in visitors, and also fear. To reach the king, a visitor had to climb the steps before the imposing palace of Xianyang, a building deliberately constructed to convey its owner's supremacy. They passed imposing pillars and soaring roofs, walking along corridors and through courtyards faced with baked bricks of grey clay. From a distance, the palace looked drab and utilitarian. Up close, visitors would see that the muted, military walls were etched with images of coiling dragons. The grey floor was tiled with patterns of swirling curlicues around symbolic solar discs. When in the presence of the king of Qin, visitors walked upon the image of the sun itself.[10]

Jing Ke, says the *Record of the Historian*, maintained his composure, exhibiting the coolness under extreme stress that had been a contributing factor in his selection. Wuyang, however, began to lose his nerve. The king was nothing more than a lone man sitting on a raised platform in the throne room. But he was the ruler of the harshest nation of the known world, and was surrounded by hundreds of his closest followers. It is possible that the younger Wuyang, who was less likely to have considered his own mortality and place in the order of things, had regarded the mission as simply one more brawl until that point, and was only now appreciating how minuscule the chance was of getting out alive.

As the pair reached the dais at the end of the throne room, Wuyang turned pale and began visibly to shake. His sudden attack of nerves was conspicuous enough to draw comments from the crowd. At the very moment so many people of Yan had died to bring about, Wuyang risked ruining the entire plan.

Jing Ke, however, laughed it off. He addressed the bemused king of Qin directly and announced that Wuyang was a barbarian from the savage tribes beyond Yan's northern borders. He had never before gazed upon so august a sight as the king of Qin, claimed Jing Ke, and the poor simpleton was finding the entire experience of being in the palace somewhat overwhelming. Jing Ke begged the king's indulgence, but the king was impatient and demanded to see the map – an order that caused Jing Ke to set down the general's head, take the map from the trembling Wuyang and advance onto the steps of the dais itself. Nobody dared follow him. Although the dais was open to the throne room, nobody was permitted upon it without the king's permission. The armed guards were outside and would not enter the chamber without the king's express order.

The king of Qin took one end of the map from Jing Ke, tugging it away from him so that it unfurled between them. Slowly, the map was revealed, detailing the new borders of the king's domain, incorporating the area of terrain that had once belonged to the Land of Swallows. As the last few inches of the map unrolled, the dagger was revealed, nestled in the final turn of the scroll.

Jing Ke grabbed the king, snatching at the end of his long sleeve with his left hand. With his right, he grabbed the knife, plunging it towards the king's chest. The king had time to react, springing backwards, his sleeve tearing off in Jing Ke's hand, the knife missing him.[11] He leapt to his feet, struggling to tug his unwieldy ceremonial sword from its scabbard. It was too long to be easily drawn from its sheath, and the king had to scurry away from Jing Ke. He darted behind a pillar while his assembled attendants watched in paralysed fascination – none of them dared step on the dais to intercede. The king had forbidden anyone to approach him without his command, and even though he was threatened by a man with a knife, his subjects remained strictly, doggedly obedient to his wishes.

The scuffle on the dais can only have lasted for a few seconds, but it remains one of the most famous incidents in Chinese history. The king's doctor hurled his medicine bag at Jing Ke, distracting him for a crucial moment, while other courtiers yelled for the guards to come. Someone, unnamed in the *Record of the Historian*, shouted at the king to put his sword behind his back, turning his belt so that the scabbard trailed behind him.

The king swiftly did so, emerging from behind the pillar with the sword drawn. Even as Jing Ke found the tables turned, the sword cut into his thigh. The king struck his assailant a further seven times, leaving him slumped bloody against another pillar.[12] Only then did the guards arrive and deliver the coup de grâce. Of the fate of Wuyang, who must have still been in the hall at the time, there is no mention.

The king of Qin brooded on his near-death experience for some time. Even if he had no reason to attack the Land of Swallows before, he certainly had one now. He ordered his army on the border to be strengthened with additional garrisons, and sent his best general to conquer the land. The Red Prince and his father led their armies ever further to the north-east, up into the province of Liaodong, where they held out for some years.

It took a while, but the ruler of Yan conceded that there would be only one way to appease the invader. He ordered his own retainers to seek out his son, the Red Prince, and bring him his head. The Red Prince was forced into hiding, pursued by his enemies and his father. Eventually, he did the filial thing and slit his own throat.

Five years after the failed assassination attempt on the king of Qin, the ruler of Yan was captured and the Land of Swallows finally conceded defeat. Elsewhere, other Qin armies had successfully secured surrenders from the few remaining states that held out against the king of Qin.

In his own way, the Red Prince had been right. Unless someone tried to stop the king of Qin, he would not rest until he ruled every land 'under heaven', from the cold wastes of the north to the shores of the eastern sea, to the hot deserts of the west and the mountains and jungles of the south. The following year, the twenty-sixth of his reign, the last remaining state recognised his authority. As the *Record of the Historian* bluntly puts it, 'Qin conquered the world.'

In recognition of his incredible achievement, the king of Qin devised a new term for himself. He combined two earlier terms for a supreme being to make a new title, *emperor*. He decreed that he was the First Emperor of Qin, a role that would endure for ten thousand generations.

The world was of course bigger than the *Record of the Historian* suspected – even as the First Emperor proclaimed himself to be the master of it, there were entire societies who had never heard of him. In distant Greece, the Achaean League and the king of Macedonia were arguing over treaty terms, and the Roman republic was fielding armies against its sworn enemy of Carthage, uncaring and un-knowing of the First Emperor's exploits. But as far as he was concerned, beyond the deserts and steppes to the west there was unlikely to be any civilisation, merely more barbarians waiting for enlightenment. One day, they would hear of Qin and call it 'China'.

Even if the Red Prince's plan had been successful, the death of the king of Qin might not have stopped the fall of the other kingdoms. The king of Qin was not necessarily the brains of the outfit – his advisers, free of the strictures of courtly life, were the ones who had masterminded his rise to power. The plan to install him as the ruler of the world had commenced before he was even born, with the contention of long-dead scholars that the world required an enlightened prince. It had proceeded with the plot of an obscure merchant to climb the social ladder, and an alliance of scholars in search of a patron who might allow them to secure their own political ends. Ying Zheng, the king of Qin, became the First Emperor with the help of great minds – his ministers Lü Buwei and Li Si, and his experienced generals. Only after his death, when his advisers were forced to find a new mouthpiece, would the extent of his own contribution become apparent.

He was a conqueror who united squabbling states, however briefly, with initial, earthly aims that transformed into ambitions of immortality. But despite his great achievement, he is remembered not as a hero, but as a tyrant. This book is his story.

O N E

The Divine Destiny

In the beginning, there was a time of gods. Coiled Antiquity, the deity of creation, burst forth from his egg with the crash of a thousand thunders, and for eighteen millennia he grew in size, forcing the heavens up away from the earth. When he finally crumbled and decayed, the pieces of his body formed new building blocks of matter, the substance of stars and worlds.

Under heaven, the first creatures had the heads of men and the bodies of snakes. Among their descendants were the people of an iron ship, who fell from the sky when heaven refused them entry. They had fought with the Duke of Thunder, a winged creature with fiery eyes. These were the days when there was still a ladder to heaven, when the snake people quarrelled in the factions of Water and Fire, and ancient deities perished in terrifying conflicts. One fell, burning, into the Evil Water, another disappeared only to flicker unexpectedly back into being on other battlefields, his body a mass of flame. In the aftermath of one battle, pieces of the sky itself fell to earth, scarring craters deep into the ground and setting fires across the mountains. The stars tilted and the rivers changed their course, but a goddess repaired it all, and all was well once more.[1]

Her journey to the sky, however, attracted the attention of other gods, who soon descended to the earth themselves. Among the five godly factions, two half-brothers caused the greatest conflict, until the land lay littered with the victims of their war. Weapons, said the ancient stories, floated on blood, while bears, leopards and other creatures fought beneath their flying banners.

The survivors turned their backs on the nine heavenly cities, preferring to dwell in five earthbound forts, subsisting on 'eye-meat', a living thing grown in a vat without a skeleton, from which flesh could be plucked, only to regrow as if by magic.[2] As time passed, they managed to cultivate the local soil, and began growing fruits and grains. One, so it is said, interbred with local human women, and soon hybrids of gods and men began to flourish. Lifespans began to shorten. Their descendants no longer lived for millennia, but mere centuries. After a few generations, it was rumoured that the gods still knew the secrets of immortality, but that they were keeping them from humans. Favours to the gods, it was said, might be repaid with rejuvenation, but none could be sure.

When another earthly war broke out among the gods and their descendants, the ladder to heaven was destroyed, making it much more difficult to leave the earth. A new weapon was unveiled, a drum that rumbled with the deafening roar of Coiled Antiquity itself, shining like the sun and the moon, harnessing the power of lightning. Its mere sound could destroy half an opposing army. In time its master, the Yellow Sovereign, brought peace to the lands under heaven.[3] During his reign on earth, the Yellow Sovereign over-saw the flowering of civilisation, the development of writing and agriculture, the building of houses and the invention of many items that humans now take for granted. He was an enlightened ruler, and his younger days as a warrior ensured that no battles needed to be fought in his later centuries.

The Yellow Sovereign called his people to assemble a 'tripod', a great cauldron-like device in memory of his victories and achieve-ments. When the device was completed, a metal dragon flew down from heaven, and the Yellow Sovereign announced that it was time for him to leave. The dragon could only carry the Yellow Sovereign and seventy of his closest companions. Other gods were left behind, much to their anguish, as there was unlikely to be another visitation from heaven. The Yellow Sovereign's own daughter was left behind, supposedly because of the heat within her body. Another deity, a warrior who could gather clouds and make rain, was also abandoned in spite of his service to the other gods.[4]

The Yellow Sovereign and the other gods did not return, and the people of the earth were left to fend for themselves. In time the magic faded, the lifespans shortened further, and the people under heaven forgot much that the gods had taught them. Earthbound kings clung to rituals and protocols and aspired to return. A legendary ruler protected his people from the day ten suns appeared in the sky. An ancient queen somehow flew to the moon. The best of the rulers convinced their peoples to work for the common good, taming the unpredictable rivers and irrigating crops. It was, like all most vaguely defined dream times in myth, a Golden Age, where humanity flourished and great deeds were done.

All of which inspired one question from the philosophers among the humans. *What had gone wrong?*

As the time of legends passed into human history, there were those who asked, if these people of ancient times were so godlike and perfect, why did everything fall apart? In the sixth century BC, Confucius said it was because of their abandonment of protocol – for there was a reason for everything, and the many strange songs and poems of their forefathers were designed to transmit information. Confucius was the first of the scholar-sages, a former civil servant who devoted his life to teaching others, creating a caste of ministers who often had a better knowledge of the past than the people they served. Although Confucius's political career was short-lived and dogged by intrigues, many of his pupils went on to find prominent posts in the governments of the day. None of them bothered to seek employment at the Centre of the World itself, at the Royal Domain where the last of the kings of the earth pretended to rule. Although the rulers of the Zhou dynasty still enjoyed nominal overlordship, their power barely extended beyond the walls of their forts, standing on the flood plains of the Wei River.

The Royal Domain had a library and a palace, and was a place of pilgrimage of scholars and nobles. It had the most impressive ceremonies and a reputation for great sophistication, but it was merely a shadow. The kings of the Zhou had been unable to control their unruly dukes for centuries. When the master of one state decided to proclaim himself king, a direct challenge to the Zhou overlord, there was nothing the supposed sovereign could do about it. The former vassal states became separate kingdoms in all but name, still paying nominal homage to a powerless 'capital' in the centre.

Something, the sages agreed, had gone awry. Confucius decided that there was something wrong with humanity – we were born with good traits that needed encouraging, and bad ones that needed suppressing. The solution, Confucius argued, was to promote a scholar class who might instruct and admonish the men of their time. Part academic, part diplomat, these teachers of men would keep hold of the ancient songs and rituals to ensure that information was not lost to later generations. However, try as Confucius might to steer the generations that were to come after him, the success of his plans depended on firm foundations, which meant that as philosophers trusted in his central assertion, that things in olden times were inherently better and should be emulated, then his policies continued. But as the decades went on and the region collapsed into the period of the 'Warring States', the policies of Confucius seemed to relate less and less to the real world.

The Centre of the World, it was said, was the fertile flood plain of the Yellow River. The vassal states huddled around it to the north, south and east, but there was more land elsewhere. The Yellow River had a tributary, the Wei, which led up towards higher ground through a mountainous valley. This area was the land of Qin, a kingdom little removed from the outlying barbarian regions. Even though Qin was one of the closest states to the Royal Domain, it was in a world of its own – life was tough, constantly under threat from the barbarians of the wilderness, and devoid of shared borders with civilised nations.

The locals had their own myths of divine destiny, carefully preserved in *Chronicles of Qin*, a document now lost but available when Sima Qian compiled the *Record of the Historian*. During the time of legends, it said, after the people had fallen from the sky, a girl descended from those early arrivals once swallowed an egg laid by a black bird and gave birth to a son. He became a servant of the rulers and supposedly did great work in organising an early irrigation scheme. For this, celebratory black flags and the surname *Ying*, 'Abundance', or more colloquially 'Winner', were conferred on him.

Based at the western end of the Chinese world, his descendants enjoyed close relations with the rulers of it. As the legendary Shang dynasty was supplanted by the mighty Zhou, it may even have been the people of the western regions who helped tip the balance of power. Although they would soon aspire to be regarded as another of the civilised nations, it is highly probable that their origins lie not with the Chinese, but with the very barbarians that were their sworn enemies. But the outlying regions of the western borders gave the early kings of Zhou something that the others did not possess in such abundance – horses.

The early ancestors of the First Emperor were prized for their mastery of the beasts that grazed the pastures west of the Yellow River. Four generations after the original acquirer of the Ying surname, we find his great-grandson literally at the side of the first ruler of the Zhou dynasty. When the Shang were finally overthrown, it was a member of the Ying family who served as the charioteer of the man who would be king. Garbled references occupy the dynastic histories for a few more generations – one member of the family, they say, had the body of a bird but spoke the language of men. But ten generations after the establishment of the Zhou dynasty, the Ying family are still to be found in royal records as masters of the horse. Their most famous member was Zao Fu, who served as the king's charioteer in a legendary ride across the known world as the ruler rushed from a distant province to suppress a revolt.

In distant Europe, an empire arose in Assyria, Egypt was riven by civil war, and Greece began to emerge from her dark age. On the steppes of Asia, western barbarians pushed at the borders of the Zhou king.

In order to protect his own domain and the nations east of it, the king hatched a plan. He conferred the westernmost region upon the head of the Ying family in 857 BC, creating him the first marquess of *Qin*, a name derived from a type of local grain. The family now found themselves forced to look west, beyond their original lands, and to struggle for mastery of a realm that had once belonged to the barbarians, and occasionally still did. Their struggles, however, would only make them stronger.

After three generations of fighting on the western frontier, the fierce warriors of the Qin Marches had carved out a new state, at a price. The second marquess of Qin ruled for only a scant couple of years; his son, Qin the Younger, was captured by the barbarians of Rong and executed. The fourth marquess, however, grabbed his territory and held it, and was made the Grand Master of the Western March.

The people of Qin had gained a reputation for their belligerence. The eldest son of the fourth marquess resigned his position in the dynasty, preferring to lead further campaigns of vengeance against the remnants of the Rong barbarians. The title passed to his younger brother, who may have tried to placate the barbarians further by letting their ruler marry his sister.[5]

Although Qin was still an outlying region, it was no longer a 'march' but a recognised domain, and its rulers were dukes. In a time when other local rulers conspired against the king of Zhou, it was the dukes of Qin who gave him support. In the mid-eighth century a duke of Qin built the land's first capital, and supposedly obtained a magical rock that could create fires that transformed into ravens. Acquiring such an artefact was a sign of a different kind of aspiration – an attempt not only to match the king of Zhou, but also to surpass him. However, any royal ambitions of the Qin nobility were soon buried under a series of court intrigues as they were forced to turn once more to their western borders.

Reading between the lines of the *Record of the Historian*, the period 715–695 BC saw the ruling family of Qin dominated by their advisers. Amid wars with two new invading western tribes, one duke was invested at only eleven years of age. Upon his death, he was succeeded by his youngest son, who was himself murdered five years later. It was only when the eldest son, the Warring Duke, returned from a prolonged campaign against the barbarians that the family line was restored and the advisers executed. The Warring Duke had none of the civilised pretensions of the rest of the royal family; he was a tough man, hardened by years of skirmishes and sandstorms in the far west. In a single thirty-year period, Qin somehow got through five dukes, but at the end of all the intrigues, there was a strong ruler once more and relative peace on the frontier.[6]

This was perhaps bad news for the king of the Zhou dynasty. Qin had served a valuable purpose as a buffer state, thinned by periodic wars that nonetheless kept the Chinese heartland safe from barbarians. But from the accession of Duke Mu the Well-Chosen in 659 BC, Qin turned its warlike attentions away from the frontier and into the civilised world of the east.

Qin focused on its own eastern borders, on a large state already torn by internal strife. The late seventh century saw several periods of heavy drought when Qin supposedly helped its neighbour, only to be spurned when a similar dry spell afflicted its own territory. Qin continued to fight skirmishes with the western barbarians, but also with its civilised neighbours. In one of the Well-Chosen duke's most famous incidents, he had to be dissuaded from sacrificing a captured enemy king to the Supreme Deity.

During the period termed 'the Warring States' by later historians, successive dukes of Qin intrigued against their rivals. During the lifetime of the famous philosopher Confucius, Qin saw five more dukes come and go; while Confucius visited most of the major states of the period, he did not grace the upstart, conniving people of Qin with his presence.[7]

Shortly after the death of Confucius, Qin's eastern neighbour gave up the ghost in 453 BC, falling apart into three smaller states, with which Qin was swift to establish contradictory diplomatic relations. However, just as Qin stood a chance of exerting greater influence to the east, the country was plunged into internal difficulties once more. A disagreement between a duke and his advisers led to a civil war, and the suicide of the ruler during a siege. The dukedom passed between the descendants of the suicidal duke's two sons, until 385 BC, when the rightful heir gained the upper hand and had the incumbent, his third cousin, drowned in the river along with the usurper's interfering mother.

With a strong ruler in charge once more, Qin gained other accoutrements of civilisation. A new capital was constructed at Xianyang, upriver from the Royal Domain of the impotent Zhou kings, who appeased their powerful neighbours with lavish gifts. When the Zhou king sacrificed to the Supreme Deity, the meat from the animals killed in the ceremony was sent to the Qin duke as a holy offering. However, if the king of Zhou was hoping to use bribes and gifts to keep Qin on his side, he was to be disappointed. There was already talk of 'reuniting' Qin and Zhou, phrased as the incorporation of Zhou's former marchland back into the Royal Domain, but in reality an annexation of the Royal Domain by Qin itself.[8] Presumably, it was hoped by the Zhou that this might be achieved by peaceful means – perhaps the intermarriage of some suitable sons and daughters, so that one could inherit both. The Qin aristocracy, of course, would prefer simply to conquer the Royal Domain as one more territory.

Removed from events by two millennia, it is impossible to say which way things might have gone. Respect among the other rulers for the Zhou king was at an all-time low, and it was only a Confucian respect for tradition that kept them from disobeying him more openly. Tradition, of course, also held that Heaven's mandate was revocable. If Heaven were displeased with the king of Zhou, then perhaps it was time for a new dynasty, just as the Zhou had once supplanted the Shang a thousand years earlier. It was clear that the duke of Qin thought himself the ideal candidate.

In 361 BC, the young nation of Qin gained the philosopher it deserved, a fugitive noble called Lord Shang. The young lord had enjoyed earlier successes as a minister in his home country, but had been forced to flee by events surrounding his ailing princely patron. On his deathbed, the prince had recommended Lord Shang to his ruler, adding that the duke would only have two choices – put Lord Shang in charge of the government, or have him killed before he could sell his services elsewhere.[9] However, when the dying prince also let Lord Shang know what his advice had been, Shang took the hint and ran.

The *Record of the Historian* is less forgiving and claims that Lord Shang was always a bad seed, and that his supposed ill treatment was the predictable outcome of earlier transgressions.[10] Whatever the true reasons behind Lord Shang's hasty departure, he left with a palpable disrespect for ancient tradition. He decided to go to Qin, a state that had been advertising for learned men to join its government. In his audience with Qin's Educated Duke (r. 361–338 BC), he began by trotting out Confucian platitudes, in which the duke had no real interest. It was only when Lord Shang dropped the pretence and began discussing harsh realities that the duke perked up. By 359 BC, Lord Shang was not only a member of the Qin government, but had drawn up sweeping plans to improve the state with legal reform. Most of Lord Shang's ideas ran in opposition to Confucian orthodoxy, and the duke was afraid that his country would once again be ridiculed as an ignorant upstart. But Lord Shang told his ruler that he could do it the Confucian way and get nowhere, or do it Lord Shang's way and actually achieve something:

> He who is hesitant to act will acquire no fame. He who falters once the course of action is begun will accomplish nothing. . . . Those who have thoughts of independent knowledge are certain to be mocked by the people. The stupid only hear of what is already accomplished, but the wise man sees what is to come before it is begun.[11]

Confucian practice had been set up deliberately to prevent people like Lord Shang from saying such things. Confucius worked on the principle that information from bygone ages, including laws, represented received wisdom, and that a wise man would not attempt to argue with such rules. The Educated Duke, however, was ready to hear a different idea – that 'tradition' was nothing more than a lie to keep the ignorant in check, and that the truly wise would do whatever was required.

Under the authority of Lord Shang, the state of Qin was reorganised. 'Ten houses', the old Chinese term for a village, now became a unit of government. The denizens of each cluster of five or ten houses were expected to keep watch and inform on their neighbours. Anyone who reported a crime would receive the same financial rewards as a soldier who brought home enemy heads from a battlefield. Anyone who failed to report a crime was cut in half. Citizens were obliged to labour for the state on public works – only farmers and weavers were exempt. Laziness itself became an offence, with enslavement as the punishment for idleness.[12]

The nobility of Qin were not excused any of Lord Shang's rules. As a battlefield aristocracy, the Qin nobles were expected to achieve palpable military results or risk being struck off the royal lists. Shang's reforms created a harsh, fascistic society of snooping neighbours and hungry soldiers – a nation whose leaders were obliged by their very constitution to attack and expand beyond their borders. Shang's reforms created a machine of conquest, but they also made him many enemies. The peasantry he could deal with: after thousands of commoners protested at his reign of terror, he had them deported to the border regions, and opposition ceased. However, he had greater difficulties with the nobles, particularly when a transgression by the heir to the throne caused Shang to order the mutilation and tattooing of his teacher and assistant.

Although Qin enjoyed great military successes, Lord Shang only escaped his enemies at court through the patronage of the Educated Duke. When the Educated Duke finally died in 338 BC, the new ruler was the Graceful Duke (r. 337–311 BC), the crown prince whose excesses Lord Shang had once contested by punishments dealt out to his tutors. The Graceful Duke had nursed his resentment for many years, and Lord Shang took the hint. Even as the Graceful Duke was installed as the new ruler of Qin, Lord Shang bolted.

Upon presenting himself at an inn near the border, he was refused a bed for the night because he was unable to provide a valid identification. The innkeeper was diligently adhering to a law that Lord Shang himself had passed, and the ousted bureaucrat left in a state of high irritation. He had even less luck across the border, in a neighbouring country so afraid of Qin reprisals that it refused to harbour a refugee. Eventually, Lord Shang was left with no choice but to return to Qin, where he led an abortive coup attempt and ended his days a captive of the regime he had helped create. The Graceful Duke ordered that Lord Shang be pulled apart by chariots and that every member of his family should be executed.[13]

Although Lord Shang's policies did not lead to a happy citizenry, they were immensely beneficial for state control. His schemes had over a decade to take effect, and by the time of his demise, crime had been wiped out all over Qin, or rather any belligerent sorts had been steered onto the front lines of Qin's many battles. Later writers would point to the contradictions in Lord Shang's policies, and the terrible climate of poverty and betrayal that his laws forced upon the population.[14]

Even the Graceful Duke, the man who had Lord Shang killed, seemed to have been tainted by his policies, invested with a love of dirty tricks and the brutal science of the possible. Lord Shang had the last laugh from beyond the grave as the Graceful Duke continued his policies, enforcing the rule of the state with ever greater severity. Qin's quest for *lebensraum* continued unabated, and in the first years of the Graceful Duke's reign, Qin armies seized a portion of land north of the Yellow River that belonged to the neighbouring state of Wei. The duke initially gave it back, but changed his mind, reoccupied it and forced the Wei colonists to move back to their homeland.[15] He followed this conquest with a far more ambitious expansion to the south-west, into the fertile basin of what is now known as Sichuan, completely subjugating the sophisticated local civilisation and making its last king a 'marquess' within the Qin aristocracy. The territorial gains more than doubled the size of Qin's lands, affording access to rich and fertile lands and opening up routes further to the south back towards the centre of China. Most crucial of these were the upper reaches of the Yangtze River, which brought Qin into more direct contact, and ultimately conflict, with the vast Land of the Immaculate, Chu.[16]

There are signs in the *Record of the Historian* that the warring states were not merely fighting, but also negotiating. Although there were plenty of rivalries to keep them busy with one another, they also shared a growing universal contempt for the kings of the Zhou dynasty. Qin followed suit, and after the performance of elaborate *royal* sacrifices, the twelfth year of the Graceful Duke was renamed as the first year of the Graceful King.

Qin's eminence as a state was rising. But its people still had a reputation for rough ways and uncultured behaviour; the Graceful King's eldest son, the Martial King (r. 310–307 BC), died after overexerting himself in a drunken competition to see who could lift

25

a massive bronze cauldron.[17] Once a small river valley held by minor nobles, Qin's borders now extended far to the south and west. Thanks to its conquests beyond the traditional borders of civilisation, Qin now rivalled the largest states in size, but did not have to share all its borders with other civilised rivals. Although Qin still endured occasional barbarian attacks, its flanks were reinforced with long defensive walls and held at natural barriers, such as mountain ranges. Now, Qin exchanged high-level hostages with other states – the distant east-coast nation of *Qi*, Land of the Devout, sent its crown prince himself to be a 'guest' at the Qin court.

The Zhou dynasty, such as it was, still claimed to be the nominal rulers of the world. The state of Qin, however, was enjoying much better successes with its own barbarian neighbours, and put its many enslaved and criminalised citizens to work on the construction of a western wall to define a boundary which the nomads could not cross. The wall was completed around 300 BC, during the reign of the weight-lifting ruler's younger brother, the Bright King (r. 307–251).

The 280s saw Qin and Qi striving to outdo each other. In 288, it was the kings of these states who proclaimed themselves to be universal sovereigns like the rulers of legend. The other countries, however, were still strong enough to resist such a claim, and imperial ambitions were quietly shuffled away and forgotten. Capitalising on contacts made when he had been a princely hostage in Yan, the Land of Swallows, the Bright King took part in a coalition against the Land of the Devout in 284, lending troops to a general from the Land of Swallows to serve alongside his former enemies in Wei and Zhao, forming a multinational invasion force.

The coalition soon fell apart as other Qin armies gnawed at the border regions of Qin's one-time allies, but the brief union had served its purpose. The Land of the Devout had been the greatest potential threat to Qin's imperial ambitions, and now it was a shadow of its former self.

There was a belief among the people of the time that the world was truly doomed. The decreasing power of the Zhou kings was obvious even to their supporters, and it was thought among some that the opportunity to find a worthwhile replacement had already passed. It was only after the death of Confucius that his disciples began to discuss the possibility that he had been an 'uncrowned king', and that the world had failed him by not making him its ruler. Matters were not helped by the discovery that a particular planetary conjunction, thought to herald the birth of the world's saviour, had only retrospectively been identified as occurring in the year of Confucius's birth and would not occur again for another five hundred years.[18] If Heaven had withdrawn its mandate from the kings of Zhou, the ideal candidate to replace them died long ago.

Such a claim had its most vocal supporters among the scholars themselves, who, as the intellectual inheritors of Confucius, stood to gain the most from his recognition as the perfect statesman. But Confucius had only seen himself as the interpreter of tradition, not as the establisher of anything particularly new, and his successors were often at odds over how he would apply his teachings to the world in which they found themselves.

In the time that would see the birth of the First Emperor, the pre-eminent Confucian expert was Xunzi, who came from a small state but pursued his education in the Land of the Devout. In the course of his career, he became a noted philosopher and enjoyed three terms as the leader of the Jixia Academy, the highest-ranking institution of learning in the eastern world.[19] The academy took its name from the ancient Chinese god of grain, and while it may have encouraged debate and produced many great minds, its presiding deity also encouraged a sense of the real and the possible. Grain was of central importance. Politicians worked to keep their people from starving, to protect themselves from diplomatic predators, to ensure that the farmers were able to take in their harvests without distraction.

Xunzi's interpretations of ancient teachings took a similar no-nonsense approach. In fact, he took the secular attitude of Confucius even further. He dared to suggest that the stories about the gods might simply be nothing more than stories. An arch cynic, he asked if it would *really* make all that much difference if the ruler did not perform the correct ceremonies during an eclipse. Was a dragon really eating the sun, or was it perhaps the shadow of the moon? And if it was just the moon, then surely it made no difference at all whether human beings banged gongs to frighten it or prayed for deliverance?

Xunzi had little time for the fairy stories of days gone by, since he saw no evidence around him of these supposed gods and their magical conflicts. Like Confucius before him, Xunzi discounted notions of the paranormal and supernatural, preferring instead to concentrate on observable phenomena. He instilled in his pupils a ruthless intellectual rigour, throwing out any arguments that rested on the myths of ancient times. Instead, he insisted that his students pay attention to that which they knew, particularly the books of history left to them by Confucius. A thousand years of *real* politics, wars and treaties was available to study, compiled by scholars with a view to educating their descendants about the past.

Confucius's work, particularly the *Spring and Autumn Annals*, had been deliberately assembled to teach through example. Xunzi agreed wholeheartedly. Confucius had hoped his accounts of earlier mistakes and diplomatic incidents would demonstrate that only the rule of the just would prevail in evil times. Xunzi wasn't so sure about that. Xunzi saw in Confucius's histories a single, unwelcome truth, that the only thing that really worked was punishment. Confucius concentrated on ritual, hoping that by repetitive actions and solemn ceremony, mankind would appreciate its responsibilities and duties. Xunzi saw ritual as only the pinnacle of a much more compelling force – law. Confucius believed that righteousness created more righteousness, and that the most important of all the virtues was simply to treat others as one would like to be treated. He valued human goodness and in fact placed a great amount of faith in it. Xunzi was more of a realist and emphasised in his classes that some humans would need to be *guided* towards the right path. Such guidance would, regrettably, involve rather more of the stick than the carrot, leading Xunzi to imbue his own pupils with a respect for rituals and correct behaviour. Ultimately, this would mean an increased emphasis on the law, particularly penal law.

Xunzi demanded that a sage ruler be tough on crime and on the causes of crime. This came to be known as 'Legalism'.

These, then, were the things that had gone wrong. In times gone past people had contended with the laws handed down to them. They had disobeyed their rulers, and the rulers had allowed too many defiant acts to go unpunished. Like the Zhou dynasty, they had continually redefined defiance in order to avoid having to deal with it.

As he taught at the Jixia Academy, Xunzi drew his students' attention away from the airy debates of gods and immortals and fixed their minds on the real world. He pointed out that, despite the supposed authority of the ruler of the Zhou dynasty, very few graduates of the academies sought employment with him. Why? Because the state was a spent force; it was useless; it accomplished nothing. Wealth, power and influence, all these things waited elsewhere, among the more dynamic dukedoms and, indeed, beyond.

The people of Qin inspired a sense of unease among the other states, but warfare was a horrific business for all. Surviving details of officers' quarters from the period suggest that the temple of the war god and the interrogation area were one and the same, and that prisoners of war were dismembered in honour of each nation's deities. Ancient records contain the cryptic phrase 'blood for the drums', a chilling allusion to an unknown ritual that formed part of ancient Chinese military life.[20]

Where Confucius had encouraged states to be run along the lines of a stern yet loving family, the circumstances of Qin led its rulers to exert much greater control. The constant threat from the wilderness had kept the country on a permanent martial footing. Xunzi called the situation of Qin 'a narrow defile'; he may have meant the thin strip of fertile land that reached out from the Wei River, but it is more likely that he was referring to the harsh realities of life on the border: 'The people are coerced with authority, restricted to a narrow life by deprivation, urged on with incentives and rewards, and intimidated with punishments and penalties. Persons in subordinate and humble positions are made to understand that only by success in combat can they seek benefits from their superiors.'[21]

Xunzi regarded nations like Qin as a threat to peace, but he argued that the true Confucian way would always triumph over barbarism. As he got older, and the Qin nation continued to conquer the regions around it, Xunzi's words began to gain a hollow note. It was one of Xunzi's own pupils, Han Fei, who first proposed the unthinkable, that maybe the way of the Qin government was not an anomaly to be addressed, but a practice to be emulated.[22] In a sense, the people of Qin took the irreligious attitude of Xunzi to extremes; when the dying mother of Qin's Bright King announced she would like to be buried with her living lover, a wily courtier persuaded her to admit that such a gesture would not be necessary as there was no such thing as an 'afterlife' into which her spirit would need to be accompanied.[23]

True enough, there were rationales that could be employed to save face, since Confucius himself had refused to discuss the supernatural, preferring instead to concentrate on the here and now. There were enough passages in the works of Confucius that might be used to support a few draconian schemes for the greater good, and Xunzi, like many Confucian scholars, knew much theory but little practice. When his position in the Land of the Devout was further undermined by political opponents, he began to consider invitations to visit other countries. One such invitation had come from the prime minister of Qin, and sometime around 265, Xunzi decided to see for himself.

His visit there is fraught with contradictions. Records of his meeting with the prime minister show predictable flatteries in abundance. Xunzi had previously written off the people of Qin as a bunch of ignorant brutes in a distant mountain valley, yet on his arrival in the state he saw fit to praise its 'unique geographical position' and the overbearing politeness of everyone he encountered.[24] But it would seem that Xunzi was only sucking up to the prime minister to get to the Bright King himself. Once in the presence of the ruler of Qin, Xunzi was notably less complimentary, retaining his deferential air but pushing home the point that Qin would never be truly civilised until it had learned how to achieve its aims without the use of military force. The Bright King listened politely to Xunzi as he reiterated his theories of good government, but the Bright King had ruled Qin for almost forty years and had little time for guesswork, no matter how noble its intentions. Despite Xunzi's reputation for enforcing harsh truths, his grasp of reality was not good enough for the Bright King. Xunzi stayed for some time in Qin, during a period when the country's borders expanded even further, but he never gained public office in the state.[25] He eventually returned to his native Zhao, where he became a voice of increasing panic about the power of Qin. Little did he know that Qin's next ruler lived in Zhao itself, a forgotten noble hostage in the city of Handan.

Long reigns are good for the stability of a country, but not for its heirs. The Bright King ruled long enough for his nominated successor to predecease him. It took two further years for a replacement to be confirmed, but eventually it was announced that the king's second son, Lord Anguo, would be the new crown prince. Such a decision, however, merely postponed another succession crisis, since Lord Anguo himself had no legitimate sons. The *Record of the Historian* claims he was deeply in love with his principal wife, Huayang, the Lady of Glorious Sun, but if they had any children at all, she had only given him girls. His concubines, however, had produced over twenty male children, including one, Yiren, born of the troublesome Xia, Lady of Summer.

The *Record of the Historian* is reticent about the Lady of Summer; she was not highly regarded, but whether it was by Anguo or his principal wife is unclear. Yiren was also considered a minor irritation, and, as was the fate of many princelings of the day, was sent as a royal hostage to another country. His name, which simply means 'the Outsider', gives some sense of his isolation.

The presence of such hostages was supposed to prevent the states from initiating wars against each other, but the state of Qin held life notoriously cheap. Yiren was sent to Handan, the capital of Zhao, the Land of Latecoming, a state whose name could be used to imply an unwelcome dawdler at the close of a party. The state had been founded on the ruins of an earlier, larger country in the region, which had been torn apart by the constant warring of the previous century.

Life in Handan could be tense for the hostages. Only a single other state acted as a buffer between Zhao and Yiren's homeland, which meant that the possibility of a war between the two countries was constantly high. Yiren dwelt in Handan in a constant state of concern about his fatherland's politics, in the company of several other princelings from other states. He must have felt abandoned; he had been sent to Handan with very little in the way of servants or resources, and could expect to meet with a gruesome fate if ever diplomacy between his host nation and home nation turned sour.

There were, however, those who regarded Yiren's situation as one with considerable potential. Most notable among them was Lü Buwei, a merchant in Handan who saw in the abandoned princeling a sound investment. Chinese tradition holds that the canny Buwei ran the figures with the help of his own father:

> On reaching home, he said to his father: 'How much return can a man expect from farming?'
>
> 'Perhaps ten times the investment.'
>
> 'And how much of a return on precious stones?'
>
> 'A hundred times the investment.'
>
> 'How much return on helping the ruler of a state establish himself?' asked Lü Buwei.
>
> 'One could hardly count so great a profit.'
>
> 'If I were to farm most diligently I would hardly get enough food and clothing for myself,' said Lü Buwei, 'but if I establish a country and seat its ruler I should be wealthy enough to pass an estate on to my heirs.'[26]

He approached Yiren and pointed out that although he was very minor in the royal house, until such time as Lord Anguo had a legitimate heir, Yiren stood the same chance as any of the other sons of catching his father's approval. Said Buwei:

> The King of Qin is old, and Lord Anguo is the Crown Prince. I have heard it told that Lord Anguo dotes upon his Lady of the Glorious Sun, but that she is without issue. And yet it stands with

her alone to nominate a successor. You have more than twenty brothers, and you are neither the eldest nor the most well-favoured, long having dwelt as a hostage in another state. When the Great King passes on, and Lord Anguo replaces him, what chance do you have against your elder brothers, and those who are closer at hand, day and night?[27]

Yiren had doubtless mulled it over himself. Buwei, however, was prepared to offer him a way out – sponsorship. It was Buwei's belief that the essence of the problem was also its solution; it was the duty of the Lady of Glorious Sun to name a successor, and since she had no child of her own, she was able to recommend *anyone*. Buwei proposed that he journey to Yiren's homeland and somehow secure the approval and patronage of the Lady of Glorious Sun.

The proposal seems bizarre, but Lü Buwei was betting on the future. He also appears to have had plenty of resources at his disposal, since when Yiren agreed, Buwei was immediately able to furnish him with finances. A quarter of a tonne of gold richer, Yiren was encouraged to acquire an entourage and gifts to send to the Lady of Glorious Sun. Buwei himself undertook the journey back to Yiren's homeland, where he arranged an audience with one of her relatives. Ancient sources disagree as to whether it was a brother or a sister, although the *Record of the Historian* believes it was the latter. Buwei was able to pass a message on to the Lady of the Glorious Sun speaking of the good character of Yiren, and claiming that Yiren was the Lady's greatest fan in Zhao. He also outlined a less flattering truth, that the Lady's position as the ruler's favourite would not last forever.

That which beauty builds is oft destroyed by beauty's loss. My lady serves the Crown Prince and is cherished, although she has not brought forth [a child]. If she were swift to bind herself to another's son, virtuous and kind, and present him as her lawful heir, then while her lord was in the world she should have peace and respect, and a hundred years on, her son becoming king, her power would not diminish. . . . For youth is the time to trade on manifold glories, lest his love fade in time with your beauty. Is not now the time to speak?[28]

Such is the blunt yet poetic speech as recorded in the *Record of the Historian*, although Sima Qian's account differs in places from that of one of his sources, the *Intrigues of the Warring States*. The *Intrigues* places some of these events in different order, and asides elsewhere imply that the negotiations and diplomacies around Yiren went on for longer than Sima's account implies. If we follow the *Record of the Historian* to the letter, the Lady of Glorious Sun wasted hardly any time at all in catching her husband at the next available moment, and entreating him to acknowledge her newly adopted son as his legitimate heir. The *Intrigues*, however, includes additional information, including a visit by Yiren himself. In that account, Buwei's obsequious addresses are not enough, but Yiren journeys to the presence of the Lady of Glorious Sun dressed in the national costume of her homeland, the southern state of Chu, and finally persuades her.[29]

Whatever means it took to sway her decision, the Lady of Glorious Sun approached the king, outlined her concerns over the succession, and delivered a stirring catalogue of Yiren's many virtues. Although she began dispassionately and calmly, her tears soon welled up as she thanked fate for her position as the queen and cursed her bad luck for not being able to provide him with a son.[30] Faced with this tearful presentation from his favourite, Lord Anguo swiftly agreed, and presented the queen with a carved jade seal confirming her newly adopted son as the heir. Lü Buwei was dispatched back to Handan with the happy news, and with a new post as Yiren's 'tutor'. Yiren, it was said, gained new-found fame as the future king of Qin, basking in the glow of new gifts and embassies from his adopted parents, and enjoying a far better standard of living in Handan. He even took a wife, and the happy couple produced a son, the boy who would grow up to become the First Emperor.

However, the story is not quite so simple. The relevant passages in the *Record of the Historian* are some of the most controversial in its many volumes. Although elements of Sima Qian's chronicle have been confirmed by other sources, and indeed by modern archaeology, there are some parts of his account that lead some historians to regard him with mistrust. Chiefly, such suspicions issue from the time in which he wrote, which was almost two centuries after the events that he described and under the rule of a dynasty that loathed the Qin emperors it had supplanted. Consequently, some have asked whether Sima Qian might have added some extra scandal to his account of the birth of the First Emperor.

Perhaps Sima Qian had a forgotten source no longer available to us. Some of the stories he tells are, remarkably, based on eyewitness accounts preserved through only a couple of generations. The infamous story of Jing Ke's assassination attempt, for example, came to Sima Qian from his teacher's teacher, who had personally known that same doctor who threw his medicine bag at the would-be killer. But the next claim that Sima Qian made in his account is strange only because it is so scandalous – it is not like Sima Qian to repeat something so palpably unlikely unless he either truly believed it, or unless severe pressure was being applied on him to do so.

According to Sima Qian, Yiren slept with a dancing girl that summer who eventually bore him a son sometime in early 259. The boy was named Zheng, which later writers recorded using the character for 'Politic', although at the time he may have gained it from a homonym referring to the month of his birth. He was given a surname, Zhao, after the country in which he was born, although this was later changed to Ying, the surname of his father.[31] Some time later, Yiren married the mother of his child, making her the future queen of Qin, and her son third in line to the throne.

But Sima Qian's account includes an additional story, recounting the events surrounding the couple's first meeting. According to the *Record of the Historian*, the dancer in question was Zhaoji, who was one of the prettiest women in Handan and, unsurprisingly, a courtesan. She was also Lü Buwei's mistress, and had been living with him at the time of her first meeting with Yiren. Flushed with his sudden rise in status, the celebrating Yiren had proposed a toast to Buwei, and in the process of doing so, made it clear that he wanted Zhaoji for himself. Sima Qian notes extreme anger on Lü Buwei's part, and his reluctant agreement to the demands of his newly promoted protégé. He also reports that the dancer was already pregnant with Buwei's own child.[32]

There is no evidence beyond the words of Sima Qian himself, and strange incidental points, such as the mystery of why the infant Ying Zheng did not initially have his father's surname. Notably, although Sima Qian mentions the pregnancy story in his biography of Lü Buwei, he does not repeat it in the story of the First Emperor. Lü Buwei certainly performed a fatherly role towards both Yiren and Yiren's son, and would be a guardian and tutor to them both, but if Sima Qian's insinuations are correct, then he was more than merely an adviser to the future First Emperor, he was his father.

Similar slurs against Ying Zheng's parentage can be found in the *Book of Han*, a much later work that includes a section on prophecies and portents of the Qin dynasty:

> In the 21st year of the Educated Duke of Qin (341 BC), a mare gave birth to a man. In the 20th year of the Bright King (287 BC) a stallion died while giving birth. Some explain the strange phenomena as follows: if your herd gives birth to a different species, one of your descendants will have a different surname. Surely when the First Emperor was born, he was the son of Lü Buwei.[33]

Such nonsense, gossiped the *Book of Han*, showed that the ruling house of Qin was already in trouble. But regardless of whether or not the allegations concerning Ying Zheng's parentage are true, there are other inconsistencies regarding the account of his early years. After dealing so minutely with the details of his parents' first meeting, the *Record of the Historian* leapfrogs entire years to a Qin attack on the nation of Zhao in 257. A Qin army marched on the city of Handan itself, and Yiren was put under house arrest by local parties intent on executing him for his homeland's crimes. Yiren, however, was able to escape with the help of Lü Buwei, who arranged for 600 gold pieces to be paid to his guards. Another source claims that the Lady of Glorious Sun had offered a reward of a *1,000* gold pieces for Yiren's safe return, so Lü Buwei, ever the merchant, had found a way of making a tidy profit for himself. But spiriting Yiren out of Handan would not be so easy – someone would have to stay behind as a decoy.

The *Record of the Historian* offers nothing further, but a Chinese folktale suggests there is more to the story. One of Yiren's servants volunteered, in the full knowledge that his involvement was likely to lead to his death. While the servant donned Yiren's clothes and made conspicuous appearances at the windows and doors of the compound, Lü Buwei and Yiren made their escape mere minutes ahead of royal messengers bringing grave news. The false prince greeted the new visitors, who solemnly informed him that the angry Zhao ruler had ordered him to be executed. Whatever description the Zhao agents had of Yiren, his servant matched it closely enough to fool them, giving Yiren ample time to sneak out of the city to safety. As all involved had feared, the captured servant paid the ultimate price for his loyalty, and was beheaded.[34]

The servant, however, had named a price for his service. Supposedly, Yiren was thereafter obliged to care for the servant's son Zhao Gao and rear him as his own along with the young Ying Zheng – a story used to explain events many decades later in the First Emperor's life. The servant, his own son and Ying Zheng's mother all seem to have had the same surname, *Zhao*, the very same surname that was briefly used for the First Emperor himself. This was not uncommon; figures in ancient China, peasants and princes alike, often used the name of their homeland as their own. We may never know what really happened in Handan, but it would appear that a family with the surname Zhao, who could have been either lowly servants or local gentry, were deeply involved in the early life of the boy who would become First Emperor.

Neither folklore nor more reliable records are able to say where Yiren's wife and infant son were while all this was happening. Somehow, Yiren's wife was also able to elude capture, thanks to her origins in 'a wealthy local family'. One wonders, if she was so noble-born, why the *Record of the Historian* had previously taken such pains to imply she was a prostitute.

The siege of Handan marked the end of a long period of Qin victories. Much to the delight of Confucians like Xunzi, the Qin army was chased out of Zhao by an army formed of allied states. Although the new coalition was not powerful enough to invade Qin itself, it did force Qin expansionism in a new direction.

Yiren did not return to Handan. Instead he made good his escape into the hands of the Qin forces, leaving his wife and presumed son among the people of Zhao. The armies of Qin rolled ever eastwards, finally reaching the pontoon bridge that spanned the Yellow River north of the point where it met the River Wei. Armies advanced into Wei and Han, and at some point the supposed ruler of the world made a stand.

From the nominal centre of the world, his Royal Domain, the king of the Zhou dynasty sent his highest-ranking minister to talk the king of Qin out of claiming any more territory. Kept waiting and eventually rebuffed from meeting with the Bright King of Qin, the minister returned having accomplished little. His one achievement, it would seem, was an unlikely assurance to the Bright King that the aging ruler of the world, a man in at least his late sixties, would not oppose him. Whether that was the king of Zhou's intent or not, he changed his mind.

In 256, when the future First Emperor was three years old, a Qin army captured two towns barely a day's ride from the capital. Despite alleged assurances on both sides, it was too close for comfort. The king of the Zhou dynasty switched sides, reneged on his non-interference policy and ordered an alliance to head off the Qin army. Before the Qin army could get any closer to the Royal Domain, a combined army containing, as Sima Qian put it, 'the elite forces of the world' poured out of an important strategic pass.[35]

Supposedly angry at the Zhou king's betrayal, but perhaps doing what he had planned all along, the Bright King ordered the invasion of the Royal Domain itself. In an ignominious reversal of fortune, the Son of Heaven was obliged to travel to the hated state of Qin in 255 and kneel before the man who was supposed to be his loyal vassal. The old man begged the Bright King for mercy, and offered him thirty-six 'cities' with a combined population of 30,000 if he would withdraw from his sacred territory.

That same year, the old king died. His people fled east and the armies of Qin wasted no time in overrunning the Royal Domain. They were looking for the legendary vessels and artefacts used by the ancient kings of Zhou to communicate with Heaven itself. In particular, they were searching for the Nine Tripods, a collection of sacred vessels thought to provide some form of divine protection to the rightful ruler of the world.

The *Record of the Historian* states that all of the Nine Tripods were recovered. Another story suggests that the Bright King only managed to acquire eight of them, and that the final magical vessel was cast into the river by his retreating enemies, or even that it had 'flown away'. Despite attempts by the fleeing inhabitants of the Royal Domain to deprive Qin of what it wanted, the Zhou dynasty's thousand-year rule was coming to an end.

Seven years later, when the future First Emperor was a ten-year-old boy playing in his mother's house in Handan, the news arrived that the Bright King had overthrown the Zhou nobility.

Despite what appears to have been initial superstitions surrounding the Nine Tripods, the Bright King stopped concerning himself with supernatural problems. The rulers of the world had lost their mandate and their power – such had to be the case, otherwise the Qin armies would never have won. Zhou was finished, and if the dead king's ancestors could not aid him at his time of greatest need, what possible help could they be now?

Perhaps the Bright King had a point. After all, centuries of feigned loyalty to the Zhou dynasty was now at an end. Qin had conquered half the known world, including its centre, and other states were falling into line. As the *Record of the Historian* put it, 'the whole world came to Qin' to pay homage to its ruler. Unfortunately for the neighbouring state of Wei, its own ruler took his time in arriving, and the Bright King flexed his new-found imperial muscles. A Qin army invaded Wei and captured what would undoubtedly be the first town of many. The ruler of Wei took the hint and entrusted his land and people to Qin's care.

There were still disloyal countries to the east – states like Yan, the Land of Swallows, and Qi, the Land of the Devout. There were many armies left to fight, but just as the exterminated Zhou had clung to the notion of supremacy long after their power had gone, the ruler of Qin seemed keen to establish it before he truly held it in his hand.

In 253, the Bright King made his true intentions known. He held a ceremony of solemn ritual deep inside Qin territory in which he communed with the Supreme Deity. Chinese religion was as hierarchical as the society itself, and only someone of equivalent rank on earth was permitted to address the master of the sky. In performing the sacrificial ceremony, and performing it in Qin territory, the Bright King announced to the world that he was now its ruler, and that the divine power of the departed Zhou was destroyed forever.

Two years later, he was dead.

TWO

The King of Qin

Lord Anguo, Yiren's father, was now the nominated ruler of Qin. As befitted a bereaved heir, he began his reign uncrowned and with many months of mourning and conspicuous public works. Criminals were pardoned, although in Qin such a magnanimous gesture hid political aims elsewhere – it was the fate of pardoned felons to be forcibly resettled in newly conquered lands. On the first day of the new Qin year (midwinter, by our reckoning), Anguo was officially enthroned, and would later bear the reign-title of the Learned King. The new ruler stood every chance of leading Qin into new victories. Perhaps he might even offer more royal sacrifices and make another grab at proclaiming himself not merely king, but emperor?

Three days later, he was dead, too.

Yiren, the former forgotten hostage child in Handan, was now the new ruler of Qin, with the reign-title of Merciful King. The Ladies of Summer and Glorious Sun were now queen dowagers – the principal wife of the departed king being forced to share her royal widowhood with the new king's real mother. Zhaoji, the former entertainer from Handan, was now the queen of Qin, and her son Ying Zheng was the new heir. But the man who benefited most of all was Lü Buwei.

The merchant's gamble had paid off. After backing Yiren's campaign to be nominated heir, and financing Yiren's public face of royal magnanimity, Buwei was now grand councillor, directly involved in the policies of the new government.

As with the early days of his father's brief reign, the Merciful King pardoned criminals, handed out noble titles to his father's loyal retainers and ordered several projects to improve public works. To the east, the last vestiges of the Zhou dynasty hatched a plot to bring

41

the new king down – or at least the king fabricated enough evidence to suggest it was true.

In the second year of Yiren's reign, Qin armies continued to advance, now into Zhao. Although they gained further territory, a solar eclipse was enough to suggest to the superstitious that a change was on its way. The Qin forces were beaten back by a new coalition of the surviving states in 247. With its armies held back from ultimate conquest once more, Qin lost its third king in barely five years. The *Record of the Historian* does not offer a reasonable explanation as to why Yiren, in the prime of life and attended by the best doctors and advisers, should suddenly keel over in the third year of his reign.

If anyone had a motive to get rid of Yiren, it was Lü Buwei himself. Yiren's son, Ying Zheng, was only thirteen years old, an age that was handily unsuitable for a royal ruler. A regency was required, and the boy-king's mother, Zhaoji, and her former lover, grand councillor Lü Buwei, were the ideal candidates. Foul play cannot be proved, but does not seem impossible.

This was Lü Buwei's chance to shine. Keen to prove himself a master in every aspect of statecraft, it was Buwei who led the army that swept down against the ruins of the Royal Domain. Related Qin campaigns ensured that communications and alliances between Qin's three closest neighbours were wrecked, and that further advances across the ruins of Chu gave Qin territory a border for the first time with Qi, the Land of the Devout. A Qin army swept down on the pitiful remnants of the former Zhou, conquering the last of the Royal Domain. Where once the kings of Zhou had claimed to rule the world, there was now only a charred region designated as the Three Rivers commandery. In honour of his loyal service to the boy-king, grand councillor Lü Buwei received part of the region as his personal fief and the noble rank of marquess. Notably, this appears to be the end of Lü Buwei's supposed military career. A mop-up operation against the survivors of an earlier conquest did not seem to be beyond his abilities, but when developments called for a better application of military skills, he was happy to defer to the generals. He had made his point; he had led an army.

His skills were better used back at court, on long-term political subterfuge. The collapse of the Zhou, although it had been centuries in the making, was still a shocking event to the people of the time; a moment of epochal closure like the last days of the Roman Empire in the West. For a state such as Qin, which had prepared to fill the vacuum long before it actually existed, it was one more achievement in the to-do list of a conqueror. For other states, the loss of the Zhou was more traumatic; even those countries that had arrogantly asserted their own right to kingship now found themselves without any spiritual precedents. Much as they may have despised their father-ruler in the Royal Domain, some nations were surprised at their sudden orphan status. Lü Buwei did what he could to rub salt into the wounds. With the states of Han, Zhao and Wei in chaos, the only potential for strong opposition lay in Yan, the Land of Swallows, and Qi, the Land of the Devout. Lü Buwei managed to arrange it so that Yan's chief minister was an ally, thereby ensuring that when he suggested that Qin and Yan collaborate in 'attacking common enemies', he received a positive answer. In the name of the First Emperor, Lü Buwei ensured that the Land of the Devout was plunged into conflict, although the fighting failed to turn up any evidence of the Ninth Tripod, the missing magical device believed to be in the possession of the local ruler.[1]

While Lü Buwei and Zhaoji ruled in his name, the boy-king studied the art of kingship. One day, he was told, he would reach manhood and become king for real, but first he would need to study with the best. During this period, if not before his investiture, Buwei began to amass an entourage of scholars trained in the Confucian tradition as scribes, advisers and consultants. Such a staff was considered wholly appropriate for a prime minister (all the prime ministers of other states had something similar) and functioned not only as a think-tank, but as a machine to generate publicity. Even if Buwei ignored his advisers (and he did so regularly), their monographs and treatises could be circulated in other countries as part of an exercise to encourage other scholars to seek Qin. These writings were not merely copied, but also collated as Buwei's own personal compendium of all the knowledge required for a ruler.

Were it not for the later scandals that brought Lü Buwei's downfall, it is likely that his monument to posterity would have been the twenty-six volumes of the *Annals of Lü Buwei*. The book was conceived as the ultimate encyclopaedia, a distillation of all human knowledge in one giant work that conspicuously bore its patron's name; in the original Chinese, it had the proud title *Spring and Autumn of Master Lü*, a deliberate attempt to associate it with the more famous *Spring and Autumn Annals* of Confucius. Lü Buwei hoped to be remembered as a similarly wise sage, but seemed unable to break free of his mercantile roots. We do not know that a single word of the *Annals of Lü Buwei* was written by the man himself, instead, he merely funded the researches and debates of his entourage and encouraged them to contribute. Parts of the *Annals* may contain anonymous contributions by other great minds, such as Li Si and perhaps even Xunzi, but it was more important to Buwei that the book be remembered as a monument to his philosophy and statecraft. If that were his plan, it was a failure, although, in Buwei's insistence that he had produced the ultimate book, we may see the first seeds of the censorious policy that would later make Li Si and the First Emperor infamous. Although the *Annals* are an interesting window on life in the third century BC, they do not represent a cogent development of Confucian philosophy, which is perhaps unsurprising considering their multi-author status. It is believed that the texts of the *Annals* also formed at least part of the curriculum for the education of Ying Zheng. When we read the *Annals*, we read the same thoughts that informed the First Emperor and his later decisions.[2]

Lü Buwei posted the text of the *Annals* in public view, hoping its size and comprehensive nature would impress. So sure was he of its perfection that he hung a large sum of gold in the marketplace, daring any passing readers to claim it by adding a single word to his perfect publication. In Lü Buwei's boastful behaviour, we can see the insecurity of a common man made good; had he any real hand in the composition of the *Annals*, he would have known that there was little chance of a passing scholar being able to form an opinion of a text he could only read by jostling and squinting among crowds at, presumably, an extremely long series of wall hangings. His declaration also demonstrated the self-assurance of the bully; if the leading minister of the Qin state announced he had written the perfect book, the chances of someone daring to offer editorial revisions were remote indeed.

Despite the nature of its composition, the *Annals* permits us a glimpse of political theory in Qin around the time of Lü Buwei's regency. Its world view occupies an interesting point somewhere between the pious rituals of Confucianism and the brutal dogma of the Legalists, people like Lord Shang and Xunzi, whom we met in chapter one. The *Annals* pays lip service to the stories of ancient kings that Xunzi was already discounting, but borrows a little from Xunzi's own thought by suggesting that the world requires a ruler, and that with the Zhou departed, the time has come to select a replacement from the other nations. In a triumph of self-reflexivity, the *Annals* argued that if the world required a sage-ruler of unparalleled abilities, then surely the king under whose authority such a book was compiled would be an ideal candidate?

The *Annals* was not merely a public relations exercise for Lü Buwei, it was a political manifesto, establishing what he had achieved in his tenure in Qin. Amid traditional decrees that rulers should be wise and teachers should be respected, there are other elements that fly in the face of the Confucian tradition. The essence of the *Annals* is not merely a boast of Lü Buwei's power, but a defence of his past behaviour. In the view of the *Annals*, a ruler of true nobility should serve as little more than a figurehead, approving the decisions made by civil servants wiser in their specialist areas than he could ever be. Buwei even offered an explanation as to what may have gone wrong to cause the end of the time of legends. Ministers, dare he suggest, ministers such as he were overlooked:

> As to the true kings of antiquity
> The occasions when they acted on their own were few,
> And those when they relied on others, many.
> Reliance on others is the [way] of the lord;
> Action is the [way] of the minister.[3]

The *Annals* also displayed a contradictory attitude towards Qin tradition – happy to cite ancient precedent when it could, but equally eager to dismiss legends and myths whenever they offered no support. Like so many other foreigners in the Qin government, Buwei had benefited from the opportunities it offered, but did not seem to have approved of the drift further into Legalism. He pushed the idea of a 'just war' and defended the use of warfare as a political tool; this in itself was a controversial attack on established orthodoxy, which held that warfare was something to be avoided at all costs. However, the *Annals* also suggested a loosening of the restrictions imposed by Lord Shang and his successors, perhaps even a return to a true sense of 'traditional values', not the thunder and lightning of myth, but a hearty respect for what really mattered – the agriculture that kept a state alive. As an unexpected reflection of Buwei's own background, he also suggested that merchants should be valued for their ability to generate wealth. Buwei's *Annals* pushed the ideas of market forces and, in their own way, capitalism.

Most dangerous was Lü Buwei's subtle assault on nobility – his own high rank being something that he had bought (he would say earned) instead of one bestowed upon him at birth. Appealing to the ancient tales that Xunzi had discounted, the *Annals* argued that the noblest of the legendary rulers of the world had *appointed* successors worthy of themselves. Lü Buwei's point, verging on the treasonous, was that inherited nobility itself should be questioned. Why, asked the *Annals*, should an incompetent ruler be allowed to govern simply because of his father? Surely it was better for a wise ruler to select his successor from among the best possible candidates? A wise king chose the best possible ministers to serve him, of course, but in the view of the *Annals*, a wise king should also choose the best possible minister to replace him.[4]

A cunning Legalist might see Buwei's argument for what it was, a steely reminder that he held the true power, and that it was in his ward's interests to ratify his decisions. Ying Zheng, however, had another teacher – a professional politician who had trained his whole life for the kind of political office that Buwei had bought for himself.

Lü Buwei's most illustrious hiring was Li Si, a former student of the philosopher Xunzi and a native of Chu, the Land of the Immaculate. Whereas Xunzi grappled with the gap between the theory of Confucius and the realities of the world, Li Si embraced it. Li Si started life, much like Confucius himself, as a civil servant, but made some famously political observations about vermin. In the privy of the officers' quarters, he glimpsed timid and fearful rats fighting over scraps of food and scurrying out of sight at the approach of a human. He saw a very different kind of rat in the royal granaries, where the rodents grew fat on an abundance of grain and took their time getting out of the way of anyone approaching. Fear of punishment or discovery made the latrine rats the way they were, whereas complacency created a different sort of rat in the granary. Character, thought Li Si, was made and shaped by experience, not by birth.

Li Si was one of Xunzi's greatest pupils, although also one of his greatest disappointments. Whereas Xunzi saw imminent disaster in the advance of Qin, Li Si saw a golden opportunity. In his farewell address to his tutor, he told him that the skills he had learned made him highly desirable to any ruler, but that it was in his own interest to seek a master who had the best resources and the highest aspirations. It was, argued Li Si, completely futile for him to while away his days in a second-rate state like Chu, concocting great ideas that the state would be too fearful or too impecunious to implement. Li Si refused to let his potential go to waste by staying in Chu – he likened his education to 'catching a deer just to look at the meat'.[5] Li Si did not want to be one of the sewer rats fighting over scraps in the twilight days of his homeland; he wanted to be one of the fat granary rats, afraid of nobody and with plenty of things to chew on. 'The King of Qin,' said Li Si to his fuming tutor, 'now desires to swallow up the world and rule with the title of Emperor.' Rather than fight it like the noble Confucians of the other states, Li Si was ready to become part of it. He followed the money.

Li Si arrived at the ideal time. With Buwei now enmeshed deeply in the regency, he was looking for someone to be tutor to the new heir, and Li Si, in his thirties and eager for promotion, seemed like the ideal candidate. Only a couple of sentences after announcing his arrival and hiring in Qin, the *Record of the Historian* describes him 'advising' not Buwei, but the young king of Qin himself – suggesting that Li Si functioned as a tutor, turning him into the embodiment of the Legalist ruler. Although history would remember Ying Zheng as the man who instituted the rule of law over all China, it is worth remembering that in his youth, it was law itself that made him.

Lü Buwei had other concerns. As Ying Zheng approached the age of maturity, he would expect to be given his manhood ceremony. Shortly afterwards, he would expect the regent to step down, and Lü Buwei would lose all his hard-won power. Consequently, Buwei delayed the manhood ceremony for as long as possible, perhaps trying to think of a way to disqualify Ying Zheng from the succession in favour of a new, younger candidate, which would require a new regency.

After serving as Ying Zheng's tutor for almost a decade, Li Si had a vested interest in keeping his star pupil alive. Just as Buwei had once manoeuvred Yiren into the right position to become king, Li Si determined to keep Ying Zheng in line for the throne. Li Si advised him to bide his time for the ideal moment when he could capitalise not only on opportunities, but on the mistakes of others. He, too, could cite historical precedents. Just as the state of Qin itself had waited on the sidelines while the feudal domains fought among themselves, the king should wait for the Qin court factions to weaken each other before making his move. Li Si pointed to the current position that Qin enjoyed: great strength, powerful defences and the coming opportunity to sweep down upon its exhausted neighbours 'like sweeping the dust from the top of a stove'. Others might currently hold the upper hand, but the king still had a trump card – he was, after all, the rightful heir to the throne, and need only wait for the right moment to enforce this.[6]

In the early days of Buwei's regency, the Qin armies renewed their attacks on other kingdoms. Zhao, however, the native land of both Buwei and his fellow regent Zhaoji, was untouched. The young king continued his studies with Li Si, and invested grand councillor Buwei with the tellingly familial title of *Zhong Fu*, or Second Father.

Having functioned in *loco parentis* for so long at Handan, Buwei's status as the king's guardian was now a matter of state record. It has even been suggested that Buwei himself encouraged the title as a means of implying that he was indeed the true father of the king, but this is unlikely. If Ying Zheng's paternity were in doubt, then Buwei's position would be less, not more, secure.[7]

The regency saw Qin plagued by locusts and poor harvests, with an outbreak of disease not far behind. Lü Buwei, ever the entrepreneur, fought the troubles by offering a noble title to anyone who could provide a thousand measures of grain for the state stores.[8] Qin was now so large, and extended so far beyond its original valley, that it was forced to admit a much heavier reliance on agriculture than before. It would need to take desperate measures to avoid another famine, and its enemies were prepared to exploit it with several espionage schemes. One, masterminded by the state of Han, planted a civil engineer in Qin, where he suggested a new irrigation scheme. The plan was to build a canal between the Jing and Luo Rivers, connecting the waterways and providing ample irrigation for new farms. The scheme was a great success, and would in years to come provide fantastically high crop yields to feed the hungry armies of Qin. The Zheng Canal, as it would be known, would have such an effect on the area's economy that it would be of paramount importance for centuries to come. However, none of that was part of the original plan. The entire purpose of the Zheng Canal was to occupy as many men of Qin as possible on a grand scheme, thereby keeping the country too busy with internal matters to attack its neighbours.

Lü Buwei's regency also saw several notable efforts by the administration to honour wealthy merchants and incorporate them within the system. Considering Lü Buwei's background, this is unsurprising – he clearly had no time for snooty declarations of traditional values or implications of inherited nobility. If someone had amassed a fortune through other means, Lü Buwei saw nothing wrong in offering them a sinecure of some description and making them part of the establishment. One such beneficiary was a man whose sole claim to fame was a long-standing business connection with the barbarians of the western frontier, from which he had built up a fortune by bartering silk for animal furs in a never-ending cycle of profit. The man was not only given a noble rank, but invited to participate in ministerial audiences. Similarly, a rich widow who continued to run her late husband's cinnabar business was honoured as a paragon of wifely virtue by order of the boy-king. The decree was signed by Ying Zheng, but wholly masterminded by Lü Buwei. His reasons for placing such an emphasis on virtuous widowhood, however, may not have been solely involved with a desire for money.[9]

In addition to the intrigues of neighbour states, Qin had internal problems within the palace. It is unclear when Lü Buwei resumed his earlier relationship with Zhaoji, or indeed if the couple had ever stopped seeing each other in secret. Considering that Yiren left Zhaoji behind after he fled the siege of Handan and was not reunited with her for some years, it is possible that Buwei and the queen mother had been enjoying more than each other's company for some time.

Ancient sources suggest a growing tension between Lü Buwei and Zhaoji. Buwei, a social climber intent on gaining power and respect, was keen to leave his merchant past behind, seemingly enjoying his newf-ound role as regent. Zhaoji, however, had other appetites. We must regard the insinuations of later scribes with a degree of scepticism, since they were written during a regime intensely hostile towards the Qin, but even so, there are many claims in ancient sources that Zhaoji was insatiable.

With their new offices and responsibilities came new intrusions on their privacy. It could be that it was simply more difficult for the queen mother and the grand councillor to spend too much time in each other's company without eliciting suspicion.

Zhaoji was by no means the first or last woman in Chinese history to attain a powerful position, only to attract accusations of licentiousness. Ying Zheng's great-grandmother, the Queen Dowager Xuan, was the subject of numerous scurrilous rumours, and was personally held responsible for an elaborate intrigue against the Rong barbarians that involved her seducing their leader, bearing him two children, and then leading the army against him, which led to his death and Qin's annexation of his territory.[10] Similar barbarian overtures would later occupy Empress Lü, the wife of the founder of the Han dynasty, and mind-boggling scandals would attend the life of Empress Wu, the matriarch of the Tang dynasty. Such misogynistic accusations continue all the way to modern times, with the most recent devil-woman in the public eye being Madame Mao in the twentieth century. Confucius himself, in his *Spring and Autumn Annals*, outlined several occasions when the actions of just ministers were thwarted by the intrigues of their masters' favourite concubines. Later historians were perhaps guided by such an example into laying the blame for political misdeeds on the interferences of women – however, what makes the Zhaoji story different is that Zhaoji does not seem to have wanted to involve herself in politics.

Unlike her historical lookalikes, the sexual warrior Xuan, or the Tang dynasty's perverse Empress Wu, Zhaoji's fall from grace is depicted much more simply, as the pining of a widow in her thirties, propelled from an uncomplicated, relatively carefree life as a well-regarded courtesan into court politics over the mastery of the known world. Nor do the historical records offer any evidence of her own feelings – all we know of her sudden betrothal to Yiren comes from the biographies of the men involved, most notably Lü Buwei, who angrily gave up his favourite bedmate to his royal protégé, presumably with an eye on his political aims.

Much of what we are told is only discernible in the evidence and accusations presented at the end of the affair. Suffice it to say, early in the reign of Ying Zheng, when the boy-king was still in his minority, Buwei hatched a plan to keep Zhaoji occupied and away from the palace. Later authors and playwrights have concocted many variations on the theme, claiming that Zhaoji demanded so much of Buwei's time that he feared their liaison would be discovered, or that she threatened him that she would expose any number of secret intrigues unless she were sexually satisfied. Whatever led up to it, the final result is stated quite boldly in the *Record of the Historian*: 'Lü Buwei, fearing that his affair would be discovered, found a man with a large penis, named Lao Ai.'[11]

The well-endowed Lao Ai was soon employed at Lü Buwei's residence, where he was asked to demonstrate his unique abilities before a crowd. In one of its strangest passages, the *Record of the Historian* reports Lao Ai cavorting at a party with a wooden cartwheel suspended from the end of his erect penis. News of this apparently soon got back to Zhaoji, who asked if she might meet such a man.

Lü Buwei offered to go one better, suggesting that he arrange for someone to accuse Lao Ai falsely of a crime sufficiently severe as to require castration as punishment. The castrated Lao Ai could then be sent to Zhaoji's palace permanently. Zhaoji, however, pointed out that the nature of the punishment would rather defeat the object of having Lao Ai in the palace in the first place, but that was already part of Lü Buwei's plan. He arranged for the accusation and the sentence, leaving it to Zhaoji to supply suitably lavish bribes to the official in charge of castration. When Lao Ai's time came, the castrators merely went through the motions of the operation without harming him, instead devoting their time to plucking out Lao Ai's beard and eyebrows, since depilation was one of the most visible signs of a eunuch. At least, such is the claim in the *Record of the Historian*, the composition of which leads some commentators not only to doubt the provenance of the story, but also whether it was part of the original book at all. Sima Qian, the titular Historian of *Record of the Historian*, was a eunuch himself, one who had been castrated relatively late in life. He thus would have been aware that eunuchs created after puberty continue to grow facial hair, and that plucking Lao Ai's beard was pointless. Such a gaffe in the text of *Record of the Historian* is enough to call the entire section into question. It seems unlikely that Sima Qian would have made such an error, suggesting in fact that the Lao Ai incident is a later interpolation by someone with a vested interest in further discrediting the Qin dynasty.[12]

The subterfuge was a complete success. The new 'eunuch' Lao Ai was bundled off to Zhaoji's quarters, where he kept her suitably occupied and away from Lü Buwei. Since Zhaoji was still a young, healthy woman, it is perhaps not surprising that she soon became pregnant, a situation which forced her to find an excuse to move further away from the prying eyes of the court. Before her condition could be known, she announced that a soothsayer had told her to seek a better climate, and moved her entourage out of Xianyang to the old Qin capital further along the valley.

Zhaoji's sojourn upriver lasted for longer than she had previously suggested. She had originally claimed to be heading to the old capital for the summer, but stayed there semi-permanently, running a household with many hundreds of servants, headed by her new-found adviser, the 'eunuch' Lao Ai.

Over time, Zhaoji began to tempt fate in much the same way she appears to have done in her earlier liaisons with Buwei. Presumably thinking herself far from the court and untouchable by accusations, she allowed Lao Ai to drop the eunuch routine. There is no note in the *Record of the Historian* of his facial hair being allowed to grow back, or the switching of the eunuch's robes in favour of better clothes, but the most obvious sign came in 239 when Lao Ai was somehow promoted to marquess. Such a promotion was a physical impossibility – eunuchs were forbidden from holding noble office, and this was the main reason that they were permitted such access and responsibility within the palace. It would seem that Lao Ai had ideas above his station, and someone was bound to find out.

There were other tensions. Back at the capital, Ying Zheng was now twenty years of age. Traditionally, this would be the correct time to hold his official ceremony of manhood, to give him the adult cap to wear and possibly an official wife, chosen from the princesses of the other kingdoms. It would, more ominously, also be the correct time for his regent to step down and hand over the reins of power to the adult king.

Something, or someone, was keeping Ying Zheng from holding the ceremony of manhood. There is no official statement in the *Record of the Historian*, but we may infer from reported events what excuses may have been used. Soon after the death of General Meng Ao, one of the prime movers of the early Qin conquests, a tailed star appeared in the west between May and June of 239, an omen of some significance. Indeed it was – to modern astronomers it is the first recorded appearance of Halley's Comet, but to the observers of the Qin court it suggested further disasters to come.[13] Soon afterwards, Ying Zheng's grandmother, the Lady of Summer, died at what must have been a suspiciously young age. Accordingly, the young king might be expected to enter a period of official mourning, and perhaps delay his ceremony of manhood.

Ying Zheng's younger brother Chengjiao met with a suspicious end in 239 when the youthful prince, unlikely to have been out of his teens, was somehow given command of an army sent to invade Zhao. The *Record of the Historian* simply states that, while doing so, he 'rebelled against the king', although the nature of the rebellion is unclear.[14] By the strict Legalist terms of the Qin state, simply failing in one's duty would be considered an insult to one's lord, so perhaps Chengjiao merely failed to secure a victory. However, although the aged Meng Ao was dead, there were still plenty of other experienced generals who could have led a campaign into enemy territory, particularly towards Zhao – a sensitive target since it was the homeland of the king himself and his mother Zhaoji. If there is any truth in the insinuations that Buwei was the real father of the king, then perhaps the death of Chengjiao was an expedient way of removing him from the palace before opponents of Buwei might mount a coup. It seems more likely that if there were a coup attempt, it might have been mounted by Chengjiao himself, which might explain the nature of his 'rebellion' towards the king, and why his subordinates were all beheaded in the aftermath of his death.

The evidence in ancient sources is tantalisingly brief. While Qin armies continued to fight distant wars in 238, the country was treated to the sight of another spectacular comet, its tail dominating the night sky. Amid such portents, a date for the king's capping ceremony, at which he would finally be acknowledged as a man, was announced. He was twenty-two.

Before his ceremony, Ying Zheng visited a place that appears as a single, simple syllable in the *Record of the Historian*. Its importance only becomes plain when we know that it was the site of the tomb of one of his most illustrious ancestors, Wu, the Warring Duke.

Wu was that same scion of the house of Qin who returned from long campaigns against the barbarians to discover that the palace 'advisers' had seized control of the government, through a succession of regencies in the name of child-rulers. It was the Warring Duke who had ordered the execution of the troublesome ministers and seized the reins of power from the courtly usurpers, seemingly instituting a return to the harsh ways of Qin tradition. It was the Warring Duke, or perhaps his vengeful heirs, who first introduced the custom of burying the living with the dead, since he was entombed with sixty-six of his supporters. The Warring Duke was a symbol of a disinherited heir fighting back against his usurpers with ruthless, calculating brutality. It would appear that Ying Zheng, the current king of Qin, reached a momentous decision at the graveside of his ancestor.[15]

The king's enemies were to be found among his regents – the aging Lady of Glorious Sun, Lü Buwei and Zhaoji all enjoyed positions of authority for as long as their dependant was still officially a child. The strange events surrounding the death of Chengjiao suggest that there may already have been a faction in Qin that wanted to replace Ying Zheng with a more pliable heir. As had happened before in the history of the Qin, it was possible that somewhere among the regents was a person who would rather kill Ying Zheng and replace him with a new boy-king who would require 'assistance'. Meanwhile, the regents themselves seemed to have fallen out, so that far from presenting a united front to the world, the Qin state was now split between two factions, both claiming to act in the interests of Ying Zheng, but both secretly plotting to retain power for themselves. A cryptic comment in the *Intrigues of the Warring States* notes:

> Everywhere in Qin, from those who hold power down to those who hold the handles of wheelbarrows, the question is always the same: 'Are you the Empress and Lao Ai's man or are you Lü Buwei's?' It matters little whether you go to the gateway of a hamlet or walk the corridors and temples of the capital, the question is the same.[16]

Eventually, matters came to a head. The severity of the punishments dealt out and the relative fates of the regents are the only suggestions we have of who was truly to blame, and even then it remains possible that history unjustly accuses one or all of them. Shortly after the king's capping ceremony, at which he might be expected to assume full responsibility for the running of the state, his reign suffered its first obvious coup attempt.

In their palatial love-nest upriver, Lao Ai and Zhaoji's relationship was finally discovered, or at least made public, since it is hard to believe that there were not already suspicions. One story suggests that Lao Ai lost his temper at a party and drunkenly boasted that he acted in place of the king's father (in other words, he was sleeping with the king's mother).[17] The more commonly accepted version implies discovery after the fact, with Lao Ai's treason only becoming clear in the light of his attempted revolution.

Lao Ai led with the biggest lie possible, and almost got away with it. Somehow, he issued royal orders, backed up with his lover's royal seal. The palace guard, the elite cavalry and the watchmen of the capital were but a few of the groups summoned to attack Ying Zheng's residence – other less likely invitees included two tribes of barbarians. Whoever he invited, Lao Ai and his palace retainers managed to constitute a fair number of the revolutionaries. Fighting broke out in the streets of Xianyang itself, with Lao Ai's party pitted against a random selection of the king's most loyal supporters. With the palace guard apparently part of the coup, the best the king could arrange was a force of his younger ministers, armed palace eunuchs and the personal retinues of two foreign nobles. It is likely that many thousands were involved on both sides, but many may have been duped by the false orders, their contribution simply one of waving detachments of troops through checkpoints, or allowing themselves to be unquestioningly reassigned to postings away from the king's side. The actual revolutionaries, aware that the plot involved the killing of the ruler of Qin, only numbered in the hundreds, and most of those were slain during the fighting in the streets. When the smoke cleared, Lao Ai was on the run and the angry king placed a price on his head of a million coins alive, half a million dead.

In the aftermath, twenty men were executed for treason, including the leaders of the palace guards, a leading civil servant and one of the lead archers. Although many thousands were punished, it would seem that even in brutal Qin they were recognised as innocents caught up in a scheme they had not fully comprehended – after all, refusing a call to arms bearing the royal seal would also have been punishable by death. Accordingly, some offenders got away with a sentence of three years' hard labour, gathering firewood for sacrificial altars and state ovens.[18] Around 4,000 of Lao Ai's servants, however, were caught in the middle. Loyal to their lord or Zhaoji herself, they had served the lovers without comment or gossip. Although their silence represented loyalty to one master at the expense of their duty to the king himself, wittingly or not, they had contributed to a coup that almost caused the death of their ruler. They were shipped en masse to the southern marches of Sichuan and forced to eke out an existence on the frontier.

Lao Ai was less lucky. Once word got out about his coup attempt and the reward, he and the remnants of his rebel party were rounded up and executed. In Lao Ai's case, he was pulled apart by four chariots. In accordance with the Legalistic rules set down many decades earlier by Lord Shang, Lao Ai's crime was one that also shamed his entire family, whether they had known of the coup or not. Accordingly, all of Lao Ai's relatives were exterminated, including his cousins, siblings, and, if they were alive, his parents. Included in the extermination order were the two children he had supposedly sired on Zhaoji herself, rumoured to have been the next boy-kings in line for the 'regency' if the coup had somehow worked out. In this manner, the king of Qin ordered the deaths of his two half-brothers only a short while after discovering they even existed. As for Zhaoji herself, the king issued a stern decree that discussion of her involvement was strictly forbidden: 'Anyone who dares remonstrate with me concerning the matter of the dowager [Zhaoji] will be executed forthwith. Their flesh will be removed from their bones . . . and their limbs piled around the city gates like a curb around a well.'[19]

Some of his advisers and associates did not appreciate the seriousness of the announcement, and unwisely expressed opinions about the trustworthiness of Ying Zheng's mother. The king had twenty-seven of them killed before the courtiers got the message – Zhaoji was off-limits, as if the king would rather believe that she had no part in the coup than the unwelcome alternative, that she had been prepared to have her first-born son murdered.

Someone's plan backfired, although whose remains unclear. Lü Buwei may have hoped to remove Zhaoji from interfering in government affairs, but such a decision involves palpable suspension of disbelief in the alleged means of removing her. Lao Ai, with or without the support of Zhaoji herself, may have planned to seize control for himself and his supposed children by Zhaoji. And it remains possible that the interfering party was none of the above, but the boy-king himself attempting to undermine the authority of his regent by promoting someone else ahead of him. If that were truly the case, then the Lao Ai affair was not the culmination of intrigues, but the beginning of one designed to bring the downfall of Lü Buwei.

The repercussions of Lao Ai's coup attempt would continue for some years. The events made the state of Qin a laughing stock among some of the other countries, and may have delayed further military conquests by up to a year. Zhaoji herself was confined to her palace, although she was eventually relocated to a residence nearer the capital as a face-saving measure. Her direct involvement in the coup attempt remained unproven, perhaps mercifully so, since proof to the contrary would have required her own son to adjudge her guilty of conspiracy to murder him.

It was not until the following year, after a mild summer and a bitingly cold winter, that the king's attentions turned to Lü Buwei himself. After decades of loyal service, as the sponsor and adviser to Ying Zheng's father, and then as guardian, regent and chief minister to Ying Zheng himself, Buwei's career was finally at an end. Although he seemed innocent of any charges relating directly to the coup, it was after all Buwei who had engineered the prolonged dalliance of Lao Ai and Zhaoji in the first place. The king angrily dismissed his Second Father from his palace post and ordered a purge on *all* foreign influences in the kingdom. Such a directive, if taken literally, would have been an utter disaster for Qin, since it would be difficult to know where to draw the line. The king himself was born of a mother from Zhao, his wife was a foreign princess, as was his adoptive grandmother. However, the king's initial ire seemed directed against the so-called Alien Ministers like Buwei, honoured scholars from other countries who had been drawn to Qin by the nation's long-standing and generous policy on hiring advisers. Three thousand such advisers were responsible for the *Annals of Lü Buwei*, and it is likely that they were the initial target of the king's campaign to rid the country of foreign influences. The truth was now out about the 'Zheng Canal' irrigation scheme recommended by agents of Han. Although it had brought prosperity to the kingdom, and may even have saved untold lives during the recent cold snap, its original intention had been to keep the Qin government too busy on internal matters to involve itself in foreign wars.

If the Lao Ai affair were the first signs of Ying Zheng exerting his own authority, he was still hobbled by tradition. He could prevent direct attacks on his mother, but diplomacy soon forced him to bring her out of exile. He initially called for Lü Buwei's execution, but was forced, once again by diplomatic concerns, to temper his anger. It would seem that Ying Zheng had a new adviser, who showed him that there were many ways to get what he wanted.

Although we can see tiny elements of Ying Zheng's personality shining through his decrees, there are also signs of a much more ruthless voice. Li Si, the maverick pupil of Xunzi, who had so boldly turned his back on popular wisdom to work for an aggressive nation, finally had his chance.

So soon after finally gaining an opportunity to run a state of his own, Li Si was now faced with the very real prospect of banishment. Accordingly, he risked his very life by standing up to the king and arguing against the banishment policy, in a masterful memorial seemingly designed to tug at the heartstrings of every possible interest group who might hear it in the court.

'Your unworthy servant,' said Li Si to the king, 'considers that this would be a mistake.' Carefully and logically, Li Si pointed out the value that immigrants had brought to the state. Without the organisational genius of Lord Shang, Qin would never have pulled itself out of semi-barbarism.

Ironically, Li Si's argument was not as logical as it appeared. He made several claims that were untrue. Contrary to his assertion, the Sichuan region had not been conquered through the intrigues of a foreign adviser, but by an enthusiastic Qin general who rejected the aforesaid advice. Similarly, Li Si claimed that the era of the Bright King greatly benefited from the advice of another foreign minister, which was not true at all. The minister to whom Li Si referred had split the Qin royal family into a feud. But Li Si kept talking, perhaps safe in the knowledge that the only people who would notice his poor grasp of history would be his fellow foreign philosophers and historians, who were unlikely to speak against his general argument. Although he did not mention it in his memorial, there were many in the courtroom who would offer silent support – the Meng family, whose late general, Meng Ao, had been a faithful servant of the king's father and whose grandsons were companions of the king, originally hailed from the Land of the Devout. Zhao Gao, another of the king's inner circle, came, as his name implied, from the Land of Latecoming, where his father had given his life to save that of the king's father. Foreigners were not the enemy of Qin, but its very saviours.

Moving swiftly on, Li Si appealed to more materialistic concerns, likely to strike closer to home with the Qin royals. Much that the king himself held dear, said Li Si, came from abroad. Ying Zheng treasured fine jade from the distant Kunlun Mountains, far beyond the western borders of Qin. On his belt he wore a legendary giant pearl, supposedly presented to a foreign ruler by a wounded snake that he had caused to be cured. As his personal seal, he used a hefty chunk of jade so large that former kings had regarded it as a fake; but it was genuine, and came from the foreign state of Chu.

The king's sword, always at his side, was a priceless antique, the Taia blade, forged by the smith of the same name for an ancient king, once again beyond the borders of Qin.[20] Li Si's rhetoric touched, fleetingly, subtly, on the accoutrements of war itself – the fastest horses and the crocodile skins that adorned the war-drums, before moving into the most convincing argument of all:

If they must be products of the state of Qin before they become permissible, then these jewels that make bright the night would not ornament the court, and there would be no utensils of rhinoceros horn and ivory as delightful playthings. [Beautiful] women . . . would not fill the rear palaces, and good horses and rapid coursers would not occupy the outer stables. The gold and tin of Jiangnan [south of the Yangtze] would not find any use, and the cinnabar and blue of [Sichuan] would not be utilised for painted decorations.[21]

Li Si's argument dwelt far longer on luxuries than on the acts of past ministers, but there was method in his madness. Wily as ever, he had silent persuaders whose help he could enlist – the ladies of the court itself, the king's concubines and wives drawn chiefly from foreign lands in dynastic alliances. How would they take to a sudden import ban on anything from abroad, including themselves? Before he finished, Li Si posited a Qin court where only local girls remained, their hair no longer fixed by pearl-studded hairpins from the coast, their earrings missing, their clothes unadorned with embroidery save that which could be sewn together by locals. If depriving the girls of trinkets was not enough to strike fear into their hearts, Li Si added that life would become decidedly more boring. He reminded the court that it was not too long in the past that the music of Qin was little more than animal cries and the clashing together of bones and jugs. Ban immigrants, argued Li Si, and the king of Qin would also be obliged to ban sophisticated instruments, complex dances and harmonious ballads in everything from love songs to the bronze chimes of pious court ritual.

After such a reduction to the absurd, Li Si threw the argument back in the faces of the anti-foreign cabal, reminding them that, of all the supposed unpleasant immigrant influences, it was only the *people* that the king was throwing out, while the trinkets of the court were safe, for now at least: 'Feminine charms, music, pearls and jade . . . are held as weighty, whereas human beings are esteemed lightly. Such is not the policy by which to straddle [what lies] within the seas and to rule over the feudal lords.'[22]

In a final flourish, Li Si compared the king and his country to the holy mountain of Mount Tai, which did not turn away the dust that blew upon it, adding ever further to its stature. He pointed to the land's mightiest river, which never turned away a raindrop. And, in a final, supremely sneaky move, he reminded the king of the forces that had originally brought so many of the immigrants to Qin in the first place. If Qin turned them away, then these smart men, these rich men, these spurned yet beautiful women, would only find new homes among Qin's enemies, with a thirst for vengeance.

With that, Li Si was gone. He had not survived a decade of Lü Buwei's intrigues without knowing the risk he was taking. If his memorial angered the king, and it was very likely to do so, Li Si preferred to be on his way somewhere else. However, he was pursued by agents of the king and brought back to the palace. There, he was informed of Ying Zheng's reply.

He was persuaded. Li Si was reinstated and the order to expel the immigrants was rescinded. It is a mark of Li Si's victory that the full text of his argument occupies a sizeable part of his biography in the *Record of the Historian*. Although he was soon promoted to minister of justice, and eventually grand councillor, his biography is silent on his further deeds for seventeen more years.

The crisis was averted and the position of foreign advisers was protected at the Qin court – with the notable exception of Lü Buwei. The Lao Ai affair marked the end of Lü Buwei's influence, but the beginning of Li Si's rise to power. Li Si had waited ten years for his moment, so seemed untroubled by waiting only a few months more. Lü Buwei probably hoped to continue to influence matters by calling in favours from the many hundreds of officials he had appointed during his career. Perhaps realising this, an order in the king's name sent Buwei to his personal fief out of immediate contact with the palace. Before long, the king sent his 'Second Father' a spiteful letter: 'What have you done for the state of Qin that merits your rule over 100,000 households south of the river? What relation are you to Qin, that We should call you "uncle"?'[23]

There was no answer to such questions; if the king had forgotten Lü Buwei's accomplishments, he was in no mood to be reminded of them. In a time when loyal Qin generals were winning real battles, Buwei's sinecure command during the conquest of Zhou probably did not impress the aristocracy, and nor did his occupation of the heartland of the Zhou rulers. As for his role as the king's guardian, family ties were a sore point in the aftermath of the Lao Ai debacle. The letter ordered Buwei and his family (he was clearly no longer welcome among the royals) to relocate to Sichuan, that same southern borderland where so many of Lao Ai's staff had been forcibly exiled.

The decree might be in the king's name, but it bore all the finger-prints of a Legalist like Li Si. Instead of assembling swordsmen and soldiers like Lao Ai, the king had removed Lü Buwei by small degrees, first from the palace, then from the capital, and now from the heartland. Lü Buwei suspected, rightly, that further orders would reach him on the frontier until his every achievement and possession was stripped away and he was left with nothing. Sensing that the letter was a death sentence in all but name, Lü Buwei took the hint and drank poison.

THREE

The Fighting Tigers

The purges went on even after Lü Buwei's death. Agents of the king spied upon the old minister's funeral and later issued further orders to anyone who had been foolish enough to attend. Any mourner of foreign extraction was henceforth deported. Any citizens of Qin so bold as to mark the passing of the king's former regent were exiled to the borderlands.[1]

Li Si's long-term plan was paying off. The old order of amateur politicians like Lü Buwei was on its way out, and the nations that Qin had not already conquered were trapped into inferior positions. Qin's advancement continued, with manufactured excuses and supposedly humanitarian intercessions, often invading one 'ally' at the request of another, and occupying increasingly large areas of land.

After decades of ascendancy, the time was now ripe for Qin to fill the vacuum left by the departed Zhou dynasty. The story of Qin is best known to posterity simply because it was the ultimate victor, but many of the other nations had their own contenders. Remarkably, most of them knew each other – the hostage exchange policy of the times ensuring that many of the players had spent time commiserating with each other as fellow foreign 'guests'.

The Red Prince's land was more interested in survival than hegemony, but other nations fancied their chances of defeating Qin and attaining supremacy for themselves. Qi, the Land of the Devout, was in disarray in the aftermath of its late king's failed bid for the emperorship, but it still stood a chance of trying again – if it could unite all the other countries in a new coalition against Qin, then the leader of the alliance would stand a chance of taking the emperorship for himself.

To the south, Chu, the Land of the Immaculate, boasted a prime minister whose bravery and intelligence could have been more than a match for Qin. In the days of Ying Zheng's grandfather, the Bright King, it was this Lord Chunshen who had organised a treaty between the two major kingdoms, advising him that 'if two tigers fight, even a slow dog can catch them when they're worn out'.[2] It had been Lord Chunshen, in 261, who had masterminded an elaborate rescue, smuggling the Chu heir out of Qin, where he had been held as one of the king's hostage/guests. Moreover, Lord Chunshen had been bold enough to look the Bright King in the eye and tell him of his defiance, and charismatic enough to get away with it. When the rescued heir became the king of Chu, Lord Chunshen became his trusted prime minister, in a tenure that saw him leading the Chu army that broke the siege of Handan in 259, and in a career high point, his appointment as the leader of an anti-Qin coalition force in 241. It is likely that, without an enemy as great as Lord Chunshen, the ruler of Qin might have become China's First Emperor a generation earlier.

However, Lord Chunshen's luck ran out in 238 when he was double-crossed in a succession struggle. In a story that bears a remarkable resemblance to the Lao Ai affair in Qin, Chunshen was dragged into the intrigues of his young lover, who planned to pass off their child as the infant heir to the dying (and childless) king of Chu. Chunshen was killed in the violence that followed. He placed far too much trust in his lover's brother, who had him killed in an attempt to hide evidence of the deception. In a double disaster, Chu lost its best politician and gained an infant ruler of unsure provenance who was 'advised' by power-grabbing ministers.[3] To the calculating Legalist minds of Qin, the time had come to take advantage of their weakened rivals. It was now or never.

The stress of the planning was taking its toll on Ying Zheng. Li Si reported that his king 'no longer finds his drink and food sweet, nor takes pleasure in his strolls'.[4] Observations of comets and meteor showers, common in the *Record of the Historian* before the year 233, ceased for the next two decades as if the administration had lost interest in omens and portents, or astronomers were too fearful to report them.[5] The king had other things on his mind and delegated the grand plan to a series of ministers, each charged with the job of furthering Qin's conquest in a different region. The ministers responsible are largely unnamed, although one is already known to us. Following his successful pleading on behalf of foreigners after the Lao Ai affair, Li Si was given a great new responsibility. He was put in charge of the Qin state's not-so-secret project to subjugate completely the neighbouring land of Han. This would involve the commission of intrigues, assassins and bribes, the preparation of soldiers and material for a conquest, and the manufacture of any excuses that might be required for it. It would also pit Li Si against his greatest living rival, a thinker against whose talent he nursed a lifelong resentment. Prince Han Fei was Li Si's former classmate from Xunzi's academy and Han was his homeland.

Although Li Si had achieved much in the Qin government, he still had issues with his old school colleague. Whereas Li Si had to claw his way up to a leading position in a foreign government, Han Fei had enjoyed an easier, albeit slower rise in his native land.

Han Fei took his surname from the Han state, of whose royal family he was a member. In the previous centuries' jockeying for power and influence, most other small states had been incorporated within the larger players. Han, a relatively minor land, probably only survived so long because of its relative insignificance.[6]

The prognosis for Han Fei's political career was not particularly good. He was not a man of action and sought no military commission. He had a stutter that made diplomacy an unlikely option, and instead threw himself into the study of philosophy, at which he excelled. Li Si had wily charm and the freedom to head abroad, whereas Han Fei was obliged to stay in his homeland, trapped in a doomed nation by the very family ties that had led him to an easy life in the first place.

Like his former classmate Li Si, Han Fei took his teacher's realistic philosophy to Legalist extremes. Where Xunzi saw an unfortunate observation, that men were evil by nature, Han Fei saw a challenge for the institution of stern laws to control this nature and use it to the benefit of the state. Where Xunzi tried to imagine a state that served its people, Han Fei dreamed up policies that would force the people to serve the state. It was, perhaps, an entertaining diversion for the privileged prince, but it was one that his classmate Li Si took to heart. After Li Si departed for Qin, Han Fei was forced to recognise that Li Si was now working for the very state whose intimidation was keeping his homeland in such a low position.

Since his speech impediment made it unlikely he would be taken seriously, Han Fei was forced to use written memorials to persuade the Han king. During the ascendancy of Qin, he sent a number of them, carefully outlining ways in which the king could be seen to be behaving in a manner detrimental to the state. Han Fei became increasingly frustrated at his lack of effect, and effectually wrote an allegorical memorial about a man whose attempts to present his ruler with a piece of unpolished jade met with cruel punishments.[7]

There were now two main power blocs among the six kingdoms. One was the so-called Horizontal Alliance, an east–west axis dominated by Qin. This was opposed by the north–south Vertical Alliance, which included Yan, the Land of Swallows, and Qi, the Land of the Devout. Much of the Han political debate of the time centred on which of these groups the people of Han should join – the Qin-appeasers of the Horizontals, or the brave resistance of the Verticals. Although Qin presented the most obvious danger, Han Fei did not regard either alliance as a good prospect – it was no secret that the ruler of the Land of the Devout also had designs on proclaiming himself emperor. Han Fei would prepare his own country to be strong enough to remain neutral.

However, the written nature of Han Fei's memorials allowed them to be preserved and circulated. Although the prince may not have appreciated it, he had readers in high places, not merely his old classmate Li Si, but Li Si's boss, King Ying Zheng himself. The perturbed prince continued to rail against the injustices of his position, especially in the essays *Frustrations of a Loner* and *Five Parasites*, in which he attacked the sycophants who kept him from steering his king in the right direction.

Han Fei argued that an average man who was presented with the opportunity to make off with a humble piece of cloth would take it, particularly if he doubted his theft would be discovered. Conversely, the greatest and most covetous thief in the world would think twice about touching a ton of molten gold, because he would be sure that the moment he did so he would cause injury to himself. Such was the underpinning of Legalism itself, that severe punishment would achieve more in the interests of the state than optimistic Confucian humanism.[8]

Tired of palace politics, and having only recently survived a coup attempt of his own, Ying Zheng greatly enjoyed reading Han Fei's works. When he dismissed Lü Buwei, he had done so in direct adherence with one of Han Fei's most famous pronouncements, that 'high officials are not exempt from punishment for crimes, while the common people are not denied rewards for good deeds'.[9] He realised, perhaps, that many of the innovations brought in at the hands of Lü Buwei and Li Si actually owed their origins to the thought of this foreign thinker.

In another essay, *The Difficulty of Advice*, Han Fei railed against the problems faced by the counsellors of an all-powerful king, ever having to choose between flattery and insult. Han Fei's complaint, informed no doubt by his own lack of influence in his homeland, was that the processes of a Chinese court, particularly one in which a monarch could enforce such draconian punishments, encouraged 'advisers' to tell a king only what he wanted to hear. This, to Han Fei's mind, was not 'advice' at all. Han Fei's observation, which would have been a criticism to a Confucian and a handy tip to a Legalist, was that 'tasks are accomplished through secrecy, and counsel fails when it is revealed'.[10]

'If only,' Ying Zheng is supposed to have said, 'I could once catch sight of this man and meet with him, I should die without regret.'

'These words were written by Han Fei,' was the laconic and sullen response from Li Si.[11]

Ironically, it was Li Si's resentment that was to lead to Han Fei's brief success in his homeland. As Qin's project to dominate Han entered a period of open assault, the king of Han needed a diplomat as a last-ditch attempt to hold off invasion. Perhaps hearing of Ying Zheng's unexpected love of Han Fei's writings, the king of Han sent Han Fei himself.

Ying Zheng was delighted. Much to Li Si's obvious revulsion, he
genuinely seemed to be looking forward to a visit from the famous
scholar. The transcript of Han Fei's memorial to Ying Zheng,
On Preserving Han, shows a cunning mind at work as the philosopher pleads his case, outlining a series of reasons why an attack on
Han would be a bad idea. Since the planned invasion was the
responsibility of Li Si himself, we can only imagine the icy atmo-
sphere in Li Si's part of the throne room, as his sovereign listened
with obvious glee to a personal performance by the great Han Fei,
much of the content of which was aimed at discrediting Li Si's own
work of the last few months.

Han Fei's argument was a masterpiece. He reminded Ying Zheng
that Han performed a valuable role as a buffer state, and was one
that had never given Qin any trouble. In fact, on several past
occasions, when Qin had embarked on one of its earlier conquests,
troops from Han had formed part of the entourage of its 'ally',
incurring the wrath of several other states, but to Qin's eternal
benefit.

Han Fei suggested that if Qin wanted someone new to fight, it
was looking in the wrong place. He dared to imply that whoever
was planning on attacking Han (that is Li Si) was doing his king a
disservice, as a more likely enemy was actually Zhao, the Land of
Latecoming. Han Fei admitted that his state was small, but warned
ominously that its cities were well fortified and supplied. The taking
of Han would not be an easy, symbolic skirmish like the battles of
old, where the outcome was determined after a gentlemanly chariot
fight by a handful of nobles. Instead, the armies of Qin should
expect to besiege every well-defended town, and a slow process of
conquest that would threaten to exhaust the Qin invaders before
they could achieve their aims. Han Fei was sure, he said, that Qin
would win eventually, but at what loss of face when plucky little
Han would fight so hard and so well?[12]

Han Fei had more for the king to think about. He pointed out
that Qin's problems would not be over even when Han was conquered, since a revolt in Han would distract Qin armies from other
conquests, and cut supply lines in the likely event that Qin found

even more excuses to advance beyond its borders. Han Fei spelled it out for him – Han was not the enemy. Qin's ultimate enemy was its greatest rival, Qi, the Land of the Devout, and to get *there* Qin would need a clear strike at Zhao, the Land of Latecoming, and to make sure that *that* would go according to plan, Qin's biggest problem was actually the vast state of Chu to the south.

Such a comment was another indirect attack on Li Si. Chu, of course, was Li Si's birthplace, and Han Fei had now cunningly managed to imply that the entirety of Li Si's efforts were directed at distracting Ying Zheng from an attack on Li Si's own homeland. So soon after the threat to expel ministers, and the realisation that the Zheng Canal had been a time-wasting exercise, Han Fei's words cannot have gone down well.

Li Si had devoted months to planning his operation in Han, yet here was his old classmate suggesting that only an idiot (or a traitor) would waste his time on such an enterprise. In fact, Han Fei went further, implying that the state of Han was the pivot around which all the era's politics now revolved. Insignificant though it might be, an act of aggression against Han would galvanise the massive Alliances into action and force a prolonged conflict. Nor were Han Fei's words an idle critique – he had come to Qin with an alternative proposal.

Han Fei outlined a programme of intrigues, bribery and hostage exchange with Chu and the minor state of Wei, in order to assure them of Qin's friendship, but also of the treacherous intentions of Zhao.

Li Si was livid, but in his reply he made sure to mention that Han Fei was a foreigner and a late arrival. Han Fei's home state, he said, was already part of Qin's problems, sitting in Qin's metaphorical stomach like something bad the state had eaten. Demonstrating palpable distress with the credence Ying Zheng was giving Han Fei's words, Li Si reminded him that he was only seeing the public relations side of Han Fei's plotting. Just as Han was pivotal to Qin, it was also pivotal to the other states. And if the state had seen fit to send its famous son to talk to Ying Zheng, it was banking on using him to sway the star-struck king. Said Li Si:

71

[His] coming here can have no other purpose than, by succeeding in preserving Han, to gain an important position in Han [for himself]. He makes dialectical speeches and well rounded phrases, and utters falsehoods and invents cunning plots, all [supposedly] for Qin's great benefit, while [actually] he spies on Your Majesty for Han. . . . This is a plan for his own profit. I have observed [his] words and writings. His vicious speech and extravagant arguments show extreme cunning. I fear lest Your Majesty may become infected by [his] arguments and listen to his harmful mind, and therefore not examine matters clearly.[13]

Li Si had a counter-proposal, that Han Fei should be retained as a hostage so Li Si himself could pay a visit to the Han court. He would do so at a time when the Qin armies made an extravagant show of deployment on the borders, although their aims should remain tantalisingly unconfirmed. He hoped thereby to scare other states into pre-emptive strikes against each other, each being persuaded that the Qin forces were acting in concert with their rivals. Li Si proposed, to steal a phrase from Lord Chunshen, that the other states should be the fighting tigers, and Qin itself should play the part of the slow dog.

With Han Fei held under house arrest in Qin, Li Si undertook his mission. However, he was refused an audience with the king of Han, and forced to submit his own arguments in writing. With nothing to show for his mission, Li Si returned to Qin, where his hated rival Han Fei was now enjoying the ear of the king himself.

Once again, we have to deal with contradictory sources. The *Intrigues of the Warring States* claims that Han Fei pushed a little too hard during Li Si's absence, accusing a fellow adviser, Yaojia, of embezzling funds, and doing so in a snooty manner that played upon their relative births. Han Fei's opinion, it seems, was that it was the business of nobles to advise kings, whereas upstarts like Yaojia (and, by association, Li Si) had forgotten their place. Han Fei objected not only to Yaojia's low birth, but also to his criminal record, saying to the king:

Examine it, Your Majesty, for he was once a gatekeeper in Liang and stole from that state. He was an officer in Zhao and was driven from that state. To choose the son of a gatekeeper who stole much in Liang, and a minister who was driven from Zhao with whom to share the policies of your state, is not an action calculated to encourage the rest of your officers.[14]

But Yaojia had the opportunity to defend himself, and did so with a speech that, to Han Fei's presumable embarrassment, mirrored many elements of Han Fei's own *Difficulty of Advice*. He noted many previous historical incidents where kings had murdered their most faithful ministers, and avoided criticism of his past by discounting its relevance to his present service to Qin. He argued that enlightened rulers should focus on results, not gossip, and in a final sting aimed directly at Han Fei: '. . . if a man has a towering name yet not one shred of accomplishment [a king should] not reward him'.[15]

However, although the *Record of the Historian* mentions the argument with Yaojia, it also implicates Li Si himself. Whatever the rights and wrongs of the personality clash, Li Si himself returned angry from the failed mission to Han Fei's homeland, and seized upon the chance to remove his rival once and for all. When Han Fei was already discredited by his failed attack on Yaojia, Li Si delivered the *coup de grâce* in a second meeting with the king of Qin.

Li Si pointed out the state of limbo in which Han Fei now found himself – discredited at court and no longer permitted to advise the king. He also noted that Legalist principles made it clear what needed to be done:

Han Fei will always work for Han. . . . This is the nature of human emotions. Yet now Your Majesty does not employ him but allows him to linger here for a long time, and then return. This is simply leaving yourself open for trouble. It would be better to punish him for breaking a law.[16]

Ying Zheng's reply is not recorded, but he seemed reluctantly in agreement. If Han Fei was only going to return home to benefit the state of Han in its struggle, then it was too dangerous to allow him to leave. But since his attitude had singularly failed to win him any friends in Qin, it was too difficult to allow him to stay. And now that Li Si was back from his mission, Qin had no need of this particular noble hostage.

Li Si took his chance and sent agents to Han Fei bearing poison. Han Fei begged for an audience with the king to explain himself, but Li Si made sure he never got the chance. By the time Ying Zheng reconsidered, Han Fei was already dead. The Historian himself, Sima Qian, later wrote that he was 'saddened that Han could write *The Difficulty of Advice*, but could not extract himself from his own plight'.

Someone who enjoyed considerably more success in escaping the clutches of the king was the Red Prince from Yan, the Land of Swallows, who had arrived in Qin during the last days of Lü Buwei's ministry. If the vague allusions of ancient chronicles have any foundation in truth, it would appear that the Red Prince was one of Ying Zheng's oldest acquaintances. Although Ying Zheng now enjoyed a higher rank, the two men had first met when Ying Zheng was a child, when both had been hostages in Handan.[17]

It might seem strange that the heir to the throne of Yan was a hostage in two potential enemy countries, but such exchanges were common at the time. In spirit, at least, they have some relationship with the 'fostering' exchanges of medieval European royalty, establishing ties of understanding with foreign powers by ensuring that some family members were raised abroad. According to the *Record of the Historian*, Qin had been hanging on to rival heirs since at least the time of the Bright King, using them as bargaining chips with each succession. After conquest, the Qin state liked to invite its former guests back, permanently. In at least one case, it had conquered a nation by the expedient method of holding its entire royal family prisoner.

If the Red Prince had not been the heir to the throne of Yan before, he was now – it was a sign of Qin's ascendancy that the Yan 'guest' was no minor noble as Ying Zheng's father had once been, but the heir to the throne himself. However, if they had been playmates as children, adulthood and politics seems to have soured their relationship. With Qin's military activity continuing unabated, the Red Prince's time in Qin was very difficult – if the Land of Swallows ever went on the offensive, his life would be forfeit. But if the Land of Swallows became too friendly with Qin, it might find itself drafted into a war against the state that sat in between them, the luckless Zhao, Land of Latecoming.

During the Red Prince's sojourn in Qin, Ying Zheng's diplomats secured a treaty with Zhao guaranteeing mutual non-aggression. The Red Prince's father sent an ambassador of his own, supposedly to 'congratulate' Ying Zheng, but in reality to ascertain his plans. After a difficult journey to Qin, in which he escaped arrest at the hands of Zhao officials, the ambassador gained an audience with Ying Zheng, at which he presented him with a thousand pieces of gold.

Ying Zheng was perplexed – he had made no secret of the fact that he had promised the Land of Swallows to its neighbour. The ambassador, however, pointed out that the Land of Latecoming was a mere shadow of its former self, greatly reduced in size and wealth after fifty years of disputes and conflicts with Qin. In the ambassador's opinion, Ying Zheng was playing with fire if he allowed Zhao to attack Yan, as once conquered, the territory would give Zhao new strength and resources. In fact, the combined might of Zhao and Yan might be enough to turn on Qin itself.

'Out of respect for your majesty,' said the ambassador with bold sarcasm, 'I am distressed at the thought.'[18]

The story, from the often-unreliable *Intrigues of the Warring States*, reports Ying Zheng's sudden agreement with the ambassador, and a reversal of his previous plan. Instead of supporting an attack on the Land of Swallows, he determined that his power was better used further weakening the Land of Latecoming that sat between his domain and that of the Red Prince's father.

But one Gan-luo, a 'minister' of Ying Zheng who was purportedly still in his teens, was then dispatched to meet with the king of Zhao, and offered an alliance with him so they could both attack the Land of Swallows. The king of Zhao gratefully handed over part of his own border region to Qin as a 'gesture of friendship' and renewed his plans to attack Yan. With the Yan alliance facing dissolution, the Red Prince was ordered out of Qin – there seemed little point in keeping a hostage to ward off an attack when one was planning an attack of one's own.[19]

Even though the account of the specific intrigues seems to have been garbled and confused, the events presented out of order and sometimes contradictory, it is undeniable that the Red Prince left Qin in a state of anger. But the exact circumstances of his departure from Qin are even more confused, since we have another account that claims he was not 'returned' at all, to use the term employed in the *Intrigues*, but rather forced to flee in fear of his life.

In an openly fictionalised account post-dating the Qin period, the story of the Red Prince instead begins with his adult stay in Qin, and a series of unspecified insults and slights delivered by Ying Zheng. Perhaps the Red Prince, and by extension his entire homeland, had presumed to hope that his childhood association with the king of Qin would lead to some form of favouritism. Considering the Lao Ai affair and the ongoing purges against immigrants at the time of the Red Prince's arrival, it was probably the worst possible time for a foreign associate of the king to expect any special treatment.

Whatever passed between the Red Prince and the king of Qin, it was enough to make the man from the Land of Swallows seek to leave. In a reversal of the account from the *Intrigues*, the alternative version has the Red Prince begging to head home, only to have his entreaties cruelly refused by Ying Zheng. The king, it is said, told the Red Prince that he would not leave until:

> The sky rains grains of corn
> The raven's head becomes white
> And the horse grows horns.[20]

With the predictable surprise of so many other fables, the three incidents somehow came to pass (the tale does not specify how), and, sensing displeasure in the heavens, the king reluctantly allowed the Red Prince to go. His consent, however, was only a ploy. He

Jing Ke's assassination attempt (a wall carving from the Wuliang shrine). Jing Ke stands at left, tackled by a bodyguard, his arms upraised. Ying Zheng holds aloft his jade disc of authority to the right. In between them sits a pillar with Jing Ke's dagger embedded in it, and the open box containing the head of the dead general. (*Princeton University Art Museum. Photo: Bruce M. White*)

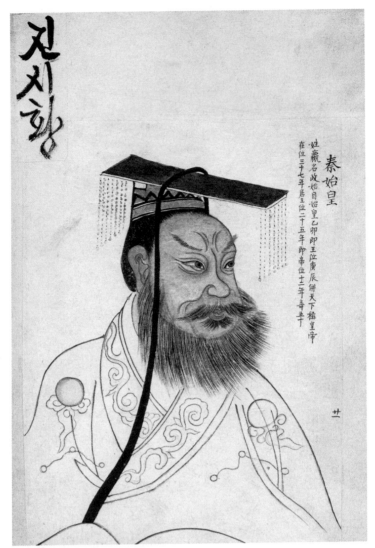

秦始皇

姓嬴名政始自始皇乙卯即王位庚辰併天下稱皇帝
在位三十七年居王位二十五年即帝位十二年壽五十

廿

The First Emperor (British Museum).
An image from a nineteenth-century
Korean book depicting Ying Zheng at
the height of his reign. *(British
Library, 4526 / Or. 11515: f.11v)*

A Qin officer. *(Photo: Frederik L.
Schodt)*

Opposite: Horses formed a vital part
of the Qin state and its wealth. These
bronze ones were found to the west of
the Emperor's burial mound, with tails
tied up to prevent them from getting
caught in the harnesses of the chariots.
(Photo: Frederik L. Schodt)

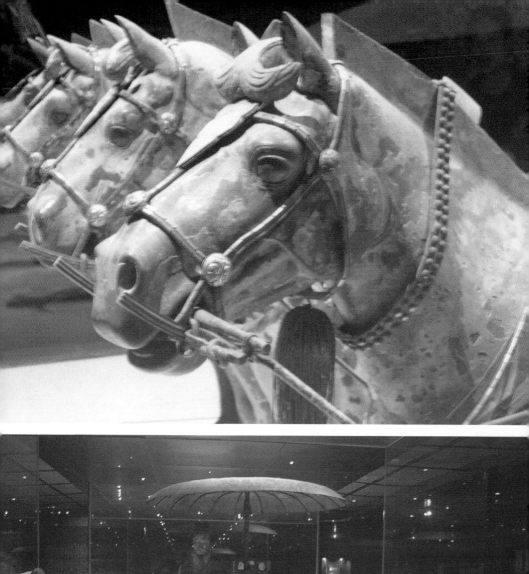

Left: Pottery in the dirt: the terracotta army as it was. *Photo: Frederik L. Schodt)*

Opposite: The First Emperor travelling in a palanquin, from a history of Chinese emperors (colour on silk) by Chinese School (seventeenth century). *(Bibliothèque Nationale, Paris, France. Archives Charmet/Bridgeman Picture Library)*

Below: The Burning of the Books, from a history of Chinese emperors (colour on silk) by Chinese School (seventeenth century). *(Bibliothèque Nationale, Paris, France. Archives Charmet/Bridgeman Picture Library)*

A Qin archer, his topknot to one side to allow the man behind him a clearer sightline. (*Photo Frederik L. Schodt*)

Opposite: The front line of the terracotta army stands to attention. (*Photo: Frederik L. Schodt*)

Pit One of the terracotta army, with its modern roof. (*Photo: Fiametta Hsu*)

The Emperor's Shadow and The Emperor and the Assassin, just two of the many modern versions of the story of the First Emperor. (© 1996 Ocean Film Co. and Xi'an Film Studio/ © 1999 Sony Pictures Entertainment)

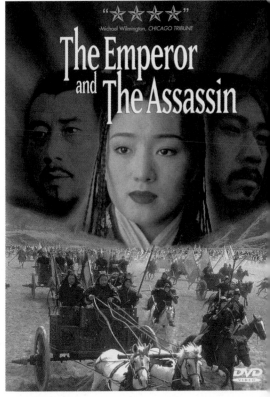

gave orders for the Red Prince to meet with an accident on his way home, a project that somehow involved a bridge over a deep gorge, rigged with a trap door set to plunge the prince to his death. By some fluke of fate, the trap failed, and the Red Prince reached it to the border under cover of the night, only to discover the gate in the wall shut. Unable to raise the guards without calling attention to himself, and unwilling to remain on the wrong side of the border until sunrise, the Red Prince supposedly imitated a cock's crow, thereby waking the real animals in the neighbourhood. On hearing the answering calls of the other roosters, the guards opened the gate, as was customary at dawn, and the Red Prince was able to make his getaway. Whether the tale of the Red Prince's remarkable flight has any basis in fact, his later acts in setting up the assassination plot testify to his annoyance.[21]

At first glance, the assassination plot of the Red Prince might seem desperate or fanciful, but Qin's designs on conquest were obvious. After decades of posturing and intrigues, Qin was able to break tradition with impunity in 230, when a Qin army marched into the state of Han and captured the king who had once relied on Han Fei to plead his case. With Han's king now a 'guest' of Ying Zheng, the once-proud state was no more, rebranded as a Qin commandery, fit for nothing more than as a staging post for further conquests.[22]

North of Han, across the Yellow River, stood Ying Zheng's birthplace, the Land of Latecoming, unluckily stricken by a drought in 229. A three-pronged Qin assault charged over its borders, only to be faced by overwhelming resistance. The city of Handan was put under siege again, while defenders fought off Qin attacks on several occasions. Faced with strong opposition, Qin's general Wang Jian used methods in the spirit of Li Si, using bribes to plant slander close to the king of Zhao that his generals were planning to switch sides. The enemy king fell for it, replacing the generals with inferior underlings, and eventually killing one and exiling the other. Within three months, the change in leadership had taken its toll on the Zhao armies and Wang Jian was victorious.[23]

The fall of Zhao is one of the few incidents alluded to in the tale of the Red Prince that allows us to date the progress of events.

By the time Wang Jian smashed the Land of Latecoming with military might and slanderous intrigues, the Red Prince's project was already well under way: the infamous attempt to smuggle the dagger in the map.

Jing Ke and his accomplice made their attempt on the life of the king of Qin in 227. In failing, the assassination attempt also presented Ying Zheng with an excuse to punish the Land of Swallows. Fresh from conquering the Land of Latecoming, Wang Jian was sent up to the southern border of Yan. The Red Prince made a bold attempt to hold off Wang Jian, but his army was defeated, and the Yan capital was razed to the ground so completely that it was uninhabited for a thousand years.[24] With great reluctance, the Red Prince's kingly father ordered his son to be executed, presenting the plotter's head to Qin as an attempt to buy some time. The embarrassment of the Red Prince's plot now dispelled, the king hoped to live on as ruler, although the bulk of the western part of his kingdom was now Qin property. The 'free' portion of the Land of Swallows now comprised nothing more than the eastern marches of the Liaodong Peninsula, up near what is now the Korean border.[25]

After long years of service to his king, the aged Wang Jian retired, handing over the command of the army to his son Wang Ben. The new general immediately embarked on the next object of Qin conquest, Zhao's southern neighbour Wei. In one of the rare moments in the *Record of the Historian* where the words of Ying Zheng himself are noted down, we have Ying Zheng's own comments on the series of conquests, which are framed as a wholly defensive exercise:

> The king of Han offered Us his territory and his royal seal, and begged to become Our subject. But then, he betrayed Us, forming an alliance against Us with Zhao and Wei, compelling Us to form a punitive expedition and capture him. This was fortunate, as it caused hostilities to cease. The king of Zhao sent his minister Li Mu to pledge alliance, and We willingly returned his hostage prince. But then he turned on Us and revolted . . . so We formed a punitive force and captured the king. [One of his nobles

proclaimed himself king of part of the remaining territory] so We sent troops to destroy him. The king of Wei first promised he would surrender, only to plot against Qin with the people of Han and Zhao in a surprise attack. The Qin soldiers and officers dealt out punishment and defeat.[26]

However, it was not possible to stop there. Now that Qin had begun its conquest, it could not afford to end.

The forces of Qin invasion were not only military. Bribes in high places ensured that the bravest and noblest of their rivals were discredited. Thanks to whispers from Qin agents, many battles were won before the first arrow was shot, since incompetent generals had been put in charge. But Qin allies went even further than military might and spies – the army also utilised the elements themselves. Ying Zheng had decreed that as the preceding Zhou dynasty had been ruled by the element of Fire, the rising power of Qin was dominated by the power of Water. Water, the reasoning went, was flexible and mighty, like the Yellow River that surged through the Qin heartland. Water was also the element that could extinguish Fire, and what better proof was needed of the Qin dynasty's superiority to its forerunner? Water, in less mythical form, was also to form a major component of Wang Ben's assault on Wei in 225. The new general ordered the destruction of the dykes that protected the Wei capital from the Yellow River. Three months later, after a decidedly soggy siege, the city surrendered and the Wei dynasty was no more.

The next country on Qin's hit list was the vast Chu, Land of the Immaculate and birthplace of Li Si. Chu's sheer size made it likely to be a tough opponent, particularly since it was a relatively young kingdom like Qin, still sporting the vitality and boldness of its recent barbarian days. The threat posed by Chu was such that not even the Legalists wanted to hear about it. When the retired general Wang Jian was asked for his estimate of the forces required, he informed the shocked war council that it would take 600,000 Qin troops to conquer Chu. Ying Zheng was not in a mood to listen, particularly since there were other generals, younger and keener on winning reputations, who disagreed.

Meng Wu, scion of another family of military men, and his colleague Lixin ignored Wang Jian's warning and led Qin armies into the Land of the Immaculate. Lixin's forces had initial victories, but met with disaster outside a Chu city that, at first sight, appeared to be deserted. The folklore version holds that with the men tired after a long march and with no obvious enemies in sight, Lixin told his men not to bother with standard protocols, which would have involved setting up minimal camp fortifications of brushwood and barricades. This oversight allowed black-clad Chu soldiers to fall upon the camp, setting fires, freeing horses and supposedly banging gongs to fake greater numbers.

Instead of defending the obvious targets of the Qin, the Chu armies went on the offensive, marching straight for Qin territory. Without the numbers to head off the unexpected assault, Lixin's army was obliged to change direction and defend the commandery or risk a cut in communications. Lixin's forces ran into the Chu army led by one Xiang Yan; as the aging Wang Jian had predicted, the Qin numbers were not enough. After suffering a crushing defeat, Lixin's army ran for three days, pursued all the while by the victorious forces of the Land of the Immaculate. According to popular Chinese legend, the victorious defenders made a virtue of their low numbers and their knowledge of the terrain, reversing traditional methods of warfare by resting during the day and attacking only at night. Unable to set up camp, and forced to guard during uneventful days and wake to defend unpredictable night assaults, the Qin army was soon winnowed down. But on the third day, when Meng Wu arrived with a weary relief force, the Chu defenders melted away again. Having lost not only face but also an army, Lixin committed suicide, leaving a note that admitted his shame to both Ying Zheng and, notably, the old general Wang Jian whom he had so cavalierly underbid for the job in the first place.[27]

Wang Jian was called out of retirement to clean up the mess. He reached Chu with considerably higher numbers of troops and embarked on a long, arduous process, capturing town after town. The Chu hero Xiang Yan eventually fell in battle, and after over a year of sieges and slow progress, Wang Jian's men captured the king of Chu. Areas of the Land of the Immaculate held out until 222, but it was finished.

Wang Jian was finally permitted to retire, and his son Wang Ben was sent north to deal with the remnants of Yan, the Land of Swallows. Wang Ben's army made short work of them, capturing the father of the Red Prince and announcing an end to the rule of his dynasty. On the way home, Wang Ben also found the time to drop in on a pocket of resistance in the Land of Latecoming and shut down another royal house.

Now Qin ruled every scrap of land except for Qi, the Land of the Devout. Although Qi had once presented a strong threat to Qin, it was no longer in a position to resist, its last hope of mounting a defence ruined by the careful positioning of a Qin agent as its leading minister. In 221, Wang Ben's victorious army marched towards Qi, where it met with only the most token resistance. The last of Qin's enemies was defeated not with some dreadful Armageddon, but with an exchange of treaties and memorials. With the fall of the Land of the Devout, the Qin dynasty and its ruler was acknowledged as the overlord of all the lands known to the ancient Chinese. Ying Zheng had become the king of kings and deserved a new title in recognition of that fact. A surviving memorial of Ying Zheng evokes his weary summation of his achievements, shortly before his fortieth birthday:

> The king of Chu offered Us land in the west [of his country], but then broke his word and attacked. . . . We sent troops against him and captured him, and with him, the lands that had been his. The king of Yan succumbed to foolishness, allowing his son the Red Prince to send Jing Ke to kill Us. Our officers and men visited punishment upon them, and destroyed their state. The king of Qi took the advice of [his minister] Hou Sheng and cut off relations with Us, so we punished him and captured him, and with him his land.[28]

Ying Zheng could tell the biggest lies he wanted, since nobody would dare to disagree. It is obvious that the attack on Chu was manufactured on the thinnest pretext, and that the Red Prince's suspicions had been entirely justified, and yet now Ying Zheng presented his behaviour as a wholly defensive act. The minister Hou Sheng, whom he blamed for the fall of the Land of the Devout, had been the self-same minister whom Qin agents had been bribing!

However, it was too late. All resistance had been quashed, and exercising the prerogative of the conqueror, Ying Zheng rewrote history to paint the kings as 'rebellious princes' in need of discipline. 'Thanks to the sacred power of Our ancestors,' he added, 'all six kings have been chastised as they deserved. All under heaven is brought to heel.'[29]

Li Si and two other ministers debated the constitutional implications. Ying Zheng was clearly no longer a king in the old sense, nor could he purloin the titles of the old Zhou rulers, since he had surpassed them in his achievement. After long debate, Ying Zheng's advisers decided to combine a series of old terms for the all-highest, including *huang*, the old term for the rulers of the world, and *di*, an archaic word for the supreme being of a departed dynasty. The final term, *huangdi*, means Emperor in Chinese to this day.

But Ying Zheng and his advisers would take things even further. One of the first recorded acts of his new imperial majesty was the renaming of his father. This was quite standard in Chinese dynasties, where deceased family members were given new titles in the afterlife, and posthumous appellations designed to memorialise their greatest deeds. However, this attitude soon ground to a staggering halt, with an edict from Ying Zheng that swept away the traditions of history.

Ying Zheng decided that his father's regnal name would be the last. He himself would not require one, nor a posthumous honour, nor any of the time-wasting distractions of traditional nomenclature. Instead, he declared that only one name would be necessary. He would, now and forever, be known simply as the First Emperor of the Qin – *Qin Shi Huangdi*. In the event of his death, his successor would simply be the Second Emperor, his successor the Third, and so on, for 'ten thousand generations'.

FOUR

The River of Power

The First Emperor's refusal of anything but the most simple of titles was met with surprise by many, although tellingly not by Li Si. As the First Emperor's tutor, Li Si was better prepared than most for the strange directives that began to arrive. While other ministers seem to have expected business as usual, simply on a larger scale, the First Emperor soon put them right.

One minister brought up the subject of administration. Since the First Emperor now had many thousands of square miles of conquered territory, he would need to delegate local rule. The traditional way to do this, as practised by the former dynasty, would be to install the First Emperor's children in fiefdoms all over the empire.

The First Emperor already had a number of children, although it is impossible to discern how many. His eldest surviving son, Prince Fusu, was either in his late teens or early twenties at the time of the First Emperor's accession. He had grown up in Xianyang, untroubled by the usual hostage exchange that threw into upheaval the lives of so many other young nobles. In his childhood, he had instead enjoyed the company of other Qin nobles – asides in the *Record of the Historian* imply that he was a long-time friend of the younger generation of the Meng family, and may have even been a childhood playmate of the great general Meng Ao's grandchildren. There is, however, little other information available on Fusu. When he appears in ancient chronicles, it is as a truly fine, upstanding statesman in the making – despite the likelihood of a lifetime of Legalist education, he appears to have remained a stoic Confucian, determined to do what was right by his loyal subjects. This, of course, was wholly inappropriate in a Legalist leader. Fusu was liked though not feared, but there was plenty of time to drum his softer elements out of him. One day, it was hoped, he would make a fine Second Emperor, although any discussion of the First Emperor's demise was taboo.

Fusu was not the only son. Nothing is known of the First Emperor's wives and concubines, but he is likely to have had dozens, from chaste political alliances to one-night bedmates. He had the pick of all the women in China, and sired at least twenty children in the course of his life. It would be ideal, suggested the traditionalists, for him to start preparing these many princelings for government. The princesses should be married off to the most trustworthy of ministers, so that they, too, would be linked by family ties to the throne. Then all the sons and sons-in-law could be dispatched to the farthest corners of the empire, there to rule in the name of their lord.

Li Si disagreed. He pointed out that the same tradition everyone was hoping to resurrect had been one of the reasons for the unrest that had plagued the world for so long. If the First Emperor installed feudal lords, then he would simply be repeating the mistakes of the past. At some unknown future date, a group of overconfident, disrespectful descendants would proclaim themselves dukes, then kings, and then eventually fight among themselves. Meanwhile, the central authority of their supposed leader would be gradually undermined, until some future descendant of the First Emperor would find himself as luckless and friendless as the last of the Zhou.[1]

Li Si instead suggested that the empire be divided into thirty-six provinces, and that each province should be managed by a government appointee. Such people were not to be chosen for their relation to the Emperor, but for their suitability for the job. They should also be removable, subject to a veto by a local political officer, and have powers separate from that of the local military commanders.

Now that the First Emperor had unified the realm by force, he also began to take steps to ensure that it remained united. As part of the process, weapons were confiscated. Officers ran amnesties all over the empire, and the quantities of bronze thus obtained were melted down and turned into a dozen massive statues in the First Emperor's capital.

With such vast responsibilities, the Qin government made the maintenance of agriculture one of its central priorities. Officials were expected to keep careful reports of variances in climate and rainfall and how the fields might be affected. Punishment awaited those who allowed the granary roofs to leak, or who permitted vermin to flourish – three mouseholes found in the walls or floor were regarded as equal to one rat hole. Retiring officers were expected to collaborate with their successors in conducting an audit of available stores. Careful notes were to be taken of the condition of tools, and losses and breakages had to be accounted for; this latter command was particularly important, considering that farming implements were a likely source of weaponry for rebellious peasants. Farm workers were discouraged from consuming alcohol – buying or selling it was considered a crime.

Prior to the time of the First Emperor, each state had issued its own coinage. Qi, Yan and Zhao had used 'coins' shaped like small knives, terminating in a round pommel with a hole in it in order to thread the money on a piece of string. But Zhao had another kind of coin, shaped like a shovel, which was also used in the neighbouring states of Han and Wei. In Chu, the local coinage was shaped like a seashell. Only a few places used coins as we might recognise them, circular metal discs with holes in the middle were used as currency in the old Royal Domain of the Zhou people, a few minor states and in Qin itself. By decree of the First Emperor, all regions under heaven were now obliged to use the Qin coinage.

Not all prices were defined in coins. The size of a 'unit' of gold was also standardised, along with other weights and measures. The Qin government issued domed lumps of metal stamped with a seal of authenticity so that units of weight would be the same all over the empire. It also ensured that whenever a buyer or seller checked his merchandise, he would see the engraved reminder of who was the ruler of all under heaven. Similar decrees established units of volume, with Qin-approved scoops issued to merchants. The immediate benefit to the state came in the ability to establish taxes and tithes all over the empire – fairness for the taxpayer was of lesser consideration than ease of access for the tax collector. The unification of weights and measures also streamlined communications across the old borders, encouraging the former Warring States in trade with each other and with their conqueror. More trade, of course, would also mean more tax.[2]

The First Emperor's Legalist background also showed in one of his most important changes, which established basic points of agreement for the Chinese language itself. Legalism placed great value on the naming of things, since categorisation allowed for the enforcement of laws. A passage in Lü Buwei's *Annals* on 'The Right Use of Names' established that legal waters could easily be muddied by questions of interpretation and jurisdiction.[3] The Qin reforms fought this by rationalising the writing system itself, demanding that all states write the pictographs of ancient Chinese in the same way.

Li Si was one of the prime movers of the project to unify the Chinese script, along with Zhao Gao, now promoted to Keeper of the Chariots, and a historian called Humu Jing, overseeing the writing of three administrative volumes that used approved characters based on an ancient Zhou dynasty model. The script was considerably simplified – many of the more complex Chinese characters were shorn of their unnecessary adornments. It is still possible, in modern times, to discern pictographic elements in Chinese characters – the Chinese word for 'horse' still retains the four legs and the head of its original pictogram, for example. Li Si's 'Small Seal' script was a large step in making Chinese easier to read, and in aiding the disparate peoples of the Qin conquest to communicate with as much ease as they now traded. A word might not be pronounced in the same way in different parts of the empire, so that a man from what was once the Land of the Immaculate might have had trouble understanding a man from the Land of Swallows, but once written down, the word they were trying to use would be clear to both.

Other sources imply that Li Si's simplification scheme went in two phases, and that in the later years of the Qin system, it was subject to further simplification by legal clerks frustrated with a script that was still too complicated – certain terms, it seems, were being written over and over by legal officers who wished they were simpler. Whatever the process, within a few years of the conquest, the inhabitants of the empire were strongly encouraged to use the new approved characters, and before long many of the pre-imperial texts were incomprehensible to the non-specialist.[4]

In order to speed up communications, the First Emperor also ordered the standardisation of axle lengths. Ruts were inevitable in all but the newest and sturdiest of roads, but the Qin law established that all carts and chariots would have wheels the same distance apart. It may seem unimportant, but if everyone kept to the same ruts, passage would be smoother and ultimately quicker and safer. The length of the axles, like other measurements, was set at a measurement divided by six, since six was the alchemical number associated with the element Water, which the First Emperor regarded as his divine protector.[5]

Now that the Mandate of Heaven had been confirmed, the First Emperor also implemented the official veneration of Water. The boiling rapids of the Yellow River were now renamed the River of Power, and water's ruling colour, the black of hidden depths, was used as the defining hue of the new empire. Flags were black, uniform adornments were black, and the magical number associated with black, the number six, became the common denominator of state calculations and measurements. Black, of course, was also the ruling colour of the Ying family, dating back to the times of legend when the First Emperor's ancestor had received a black flag from an ancient ruler. Although the Legalists claimed to have no interest in matters of the supernatural, someone at court was still superstitious enough to promote such gestures to tradition.

One passage in the *Record of the Historian* still divides scholars, since it claims that the First Emperor renamed his subjects 'the black-headed people'. The term becomes relatively common in later dynastic histories, and is often presumed to refer to the Qin dynasty's ruling colour – perhaps loyal subjects of the First Emperor were entitled to wear black hats or bandanas. Another possibility may have more to do with the racial attitudes of Qin's western frontier. The 'black-headed people' may have been named in direct opposition to the people with brown or reddish hair on the barbarian frontier – although the upstart Qin was acknowledged as the ruler of the civilised world, it still defined the Us and Them of its boundaries in terms of the many half-forgotten conflicts of its days as a borderland garrison.

The broad strokes of the First Emperor's initial decrees are borne out by many hundreds of other forms of state control. Historians have always known of the road building and unities of weights and measures. The modern Chinese language owes at least part of its appearance to the reforms of the First Emperor. But it is only recently that we have begun truly to appreciate what life was like under the First Emperor. For once the empire was unified and rule was established, all under heaven was forced to abide by the thing that the Legalists prized above everything else: their laws.

One particular individual is more important than any other in aiding our understanding of the Qin legal system. His name was Xi, literally 'Happy', and he was born at roughly the same time as Ying Zheng himself. Aged eighteen, he joined the Qin government as a scribe in the early days of the ascendancy of Li Si, and was promoted to prefectural clerk during the period that Lü Buwei's scribes completed the bulk of the work on the *Annals*. In 235, amid the paranoia of the anti-immigrant debate in Qin, court opinion favoured local men for a time, leading to Xi's appointment as a court judge when he was only twenty-seven years old. Judge Xi served the Qin government in this capacity for nearly two decades until his early death in his forties. He is not mentioned in the *Record of the Historian*, nor in the *Intrigues of the Warring States*. There is no record of him going into battle, and he is not remembered for any particular legal precedent or famous cases. In fact, Judge Xi was completely forgotten for two millennia, until 1975, when workers digging a drainage canal in China's Hebei province unwittingly smashed their shovels into his grave. When rescue archaeologists sifted through the remains, they discovered that Judge Xi had been buried with an entire library. As befitted an eminent judiciary official, Judge Xi went into the afterlife armed with a complete set of the Qin legal codes and administrative documents, a veritable forest of bamboo strips, their leather bindings long since decayed.

These codes, it is presumed, were the culmination of a long tradition of scholarship – we should not assume that they were created in a frenzy of legislation during the lifetime of the First Emperor, but rather compiled and modified over several centuries. However, as Qin editions, they still tell us much about life in the Qin state.

Although Legalism has gained a reputation as a Machiavellian philosophy concerning the acquisition of power for its own sake and at all costs, the letter of its law is remarkably egalitarian. Apologists for Legalism might argue that, although it is a system of fascist dogma, at least all are equal before it. However, even in Legalism's earliest days, Lord Shang was forced to compromise his belief – the successor king who brought about the death of Lord Shang should not have been permitted to live under the full force of Shang's laws. It would seem that by the time of Ying Zheng, the brutal codes of Legalism had already developed a new, pragmatic appendix. A Legalist state lived for the law itself, the laws defined the very models of behaviour, and served also as the acquisitory engines of more power and wealth. Criminals were allowed, indeed encouraged, to buy their way out of sentences, since the payment of a fine was of more use to the state than a vengeful punitive injury such as castration, mutilation or tattooing. In this, Qin was not unique, and nor were other states in antiquity. Long before the rise of Qin, similar codes of conduct had been established elsewhere, in Mesopotamia for example, where law was also established for economic reasons.[6] Such get-out clauses even affected the more draconian crimes, so that if a convict was sentenced to hard labour or slavery, he was encouraged to hire proxies to carry out his sentence for him. The Qin government would relieve a man of his enslavement if he could provide four others (or the price of four others) to take his place. It was a win-win situation for the Qin state, since at the worst case scenario it would gain one new labourer on state enterprises, whereas at the best case it would gain four, all for the bringing of 'justice' to a single case.[7] Similarly, bondservants could redeem themselves by providing two alternate adults to do their work. Aging bondservants or minors could be swapped for an able-bodied, healthy adult. Persons of higher social rank were able to demote themselves by two grades in order to redeem a family member from a crime, making social standing itself part of the currency of justice.

Although the First Emperor maintained that all the nations were now unified, he was unable to avoid bad feeling against him among the conquered peoples. There are allusions in the *Record of the Historian* to a series of purges in the conquered states, as the Qin authorities hunted down anyone who whispered of resistance. Justice appears to have been particularly rough in Yan, the Land of Swallows, since it was the nerve centre of the Red Prince's conspiracy, and rightly believed to be a hotbed of anti-Qin feeling.

One man who fled the Land of Swallows was Gao Jianli, the musician who had played while Jing Ke had sung his farewell song at the border six years earlier. With Qin investigators ruthlessly gathering details of any surviving conspirators, Gao Jianli adopted a new name and hid any indicators of his past life. Despite being a renowned musician, he swore never to play again, and eventually found a job as a barman in the home of a noble family.

His professional pride, however, was something he was unable to hide, and eventually he was overheard muttering that his master's entertainers were poor excuses for musicians. Following audience demands to prove it, he donned his best robes, retrieved his dulcimer and played for the crowd. His performance was so widely regarded that he was promoted to the highest available office in his new employment and recommenced his musical career.

News of this eventually reached the Qin investigators, who established that the mystery musician was indeed Gao Jianli, infamous accomplice of the assassin Jing Ke. He was dragged before the First Emperor, who was suitably charmed with his musical skills to grant him a pardon and keep him as an entertainer. To keep Gao Jianli from acting on his rebellious impulses, the musician was blinded with acid. However, this was not enough to prevent him attempting to avenge Jing Ke and his country. At some later date, perhaps 220 or 219, the eyeless musician had lulled the First Emperor into a false sense of security and found himself playing his dulcimer close enough to be within reach of him. Sensing that it was now or never, Gao Jianli leapt up, hefted his instrument and clubbed the First Emperor with it, revealing that one end had been filled with lead in order to turn it into an impromptu weapon. The First Emperor easily evaded the desperate attack of the blinded musician, and Gao Jianli was immediately executed. But another assassination attempt so soon after the first left the First Emperor unwilling to allow any subjects from the conquered nations into his inner sanctum.[8]

This directive, probably barked out in the heat of the moment, only seems to have applied to new arrivals: it is unlikely that the First Emperor's bedmates were suddenly restricted to Qin girls, for example. Nor did it apply to his advisers, since his trusted inner circle comprised Li Si (a native of the Land of the Immaculate), the brothers Meng Tian and Meng Yi (born and bred in Qin, but with ancestors from the Land of the Devout) and Zhao Gao, from the Land of Latecoming. However, the advisers, while deferential to their ruler, seem to have quarrelled among themselves.

The Meng brothers enjoyed a high status born of their family's long military service to the Qin royal family. At some point in the past, however, they had been instrumental in uncovering an unspecified scandal in which Zhao Gao was implicated. Although the details are unclear, it left Zhao Gao and Meng Yi at each other's throats for the rest of their lives. The incident may have even led to Zhao Gao's punitive castration – he is recorded as a eunuch in the *Record of the Historian*, but it is not specified whether he was castrated early in life to become the king's personal servant, or later on. He is also recorded as the father of at least one child, possibly through adoption or through conception achieved before his unfortunate castration. Whatever the truth of the matter, Zhao Gao enjoyed a charmed status as the king's lifelong associate, perhaps even step-brother. In the early days of the imperial administration, many believed that the military class were now on the wane, and Zhao Gao may have enjoyed his relative rise in status as administration and policy-making began to enjoy greater importance. His gradually increasing powers would make him a powerful enemy, and one with an eye on ruining the Meng family for good. By luck or judgement, the advisers began to polarise into two factions: one of Zhao Gao and Li Si, the other comprising the Meng brothers and their friend, the heir apparent Prince Fusu.[9]

The stark difference between official harmony and real-life tension was not restricted to the First Emperor's immediate circle. While the laws of the Qin state purported to represent all citizens equally, it was clear that some (the rich) were more equal than others. The difference with a Legalist state was that the existence of such loopholes was not a crime in itself – instead, the brutal pragmatism of Legalism acknowledged that it was possible to buy one's way out of trouble.

Evidence of such problems can be found in the grave of Judge Xi. The archaeologists did not merely find laws. They also found detailed procedural documents, outlining the models for the interrogation of suspects and witnesses. Qin legal officials were advised to take separate statements, and not to influence their initial claims:

When his statement has been completely noted down, and it cannot be understood, then insist on the points [which need] insisting. When, having insisted, one has again fully listened and noted down the explanatory statements, one looks again at other unexplained points and insists again on these.[10]

The facetious logic of the Legalist procedures was open to abuse. If a suspect's story was still not acceptable, his interrogators were authorised to torture him until his statement was satisfactory. While the documents are crystal clear on the procedure, they offer no suggestion as to what might happen if an interrogator and his suspect disagreed on the nature of truth itself. In an even more sinister turn of events, although Qin officials were discouraged from using torture, the laws imply that it is theoretically acceptable to use it in their extraction of agreeable statements from *witnesses*, and not merely the accused.

Judge Xi's rule books contain several model cases, presumably based, like their modern equivalents, on real legal decisions. The stories they present show us much about life under the Qin – during his tenure, Judge Xi had to deal with problems of a deceptively modern nature: thefts, crimes of passion and disputes over contracts. Qin rules on public conduct display hallmarks of a land in a state of constant war. Scaremongers and propagandists who spoke in favour of enemy states were to be cut in two. Incest was a capital offence, even between half-siblings. A woman was not considered to be a guilty party if two men fought over her and one of them was killed. In the case of a slave raping his mistress, the slave would be executed.

Others are even more alien to modern eyes. There is the case of an 'absconder', a man drafted in to serve on a work-gang building a Qin palace who deserted his post. After living a fugitive existence for five months, he eventually turned himself in as part of a plea-bargain for a more lenient sentence.[11] Similar attempts to offset the severity of punishment are reported in another case, in which a nobleman turns himself in for a crime of robbery, offering instead to implicate his accomplice. Tellingly, however, the accomplice is a commoner, and therefore presumably less able to buy his way out of trouble.

A noteworthy point in the cases is the nature of the arresting officials. Although Qin had armies and militia, the onus for much everyday policing lay with one's neighbours. In one case, a man makes a citizen's arrest of a murderer, hoping thereby to gain some leeway when he himself confesses to earlier stealing an ox. In another, investigators are called to the scene where robbers have tunnelled into a man's house and stolen a gown made by his wife; the procedural records note that the robbers' footprints appeared to be of old shoes, and also that the man's estimate of the value of the gown was, to some extent, corroborated after his neighbours were interrogated.[12]

Judge Xi's lists of legal precedents included the case of criminals caught making counterfeit coins from low-grade metals; a horse-thief identified by foolishly donning the expensive and distinctive clothes he finds in the stolen saddlebag; and a uniquely grisly case in which a soldier, expecting to claim a reward by presenting the head of a slain enemy, finds that a passing ruffian has made off with the head, hoping thereby to claim the money for himself.

In an even more chilling glimpse of Qin attitudes, we find a case in Judge Xi's collection where two local militiamen quarrel over the rights to an enemy's head. Their interrogator realises that members of their platoon are missing, and appear to have been murdered and beheaded so that their traitorous colleagues could pretend that their heads were those of enemy soldiers.[13]

One case involves a village headman applying for permission to mutilate a woman. The woman in question is a slave who refuses to follow orders, whose owner wished to mark her with tattoos and cut off her nose as a punishment. The savagery of this unnamed slave's treatment is bad enough, but it is also notable that Judge Xi's legal precedents are not concerned with preventing her punishment, but merely in the necessary documentation required to enforce it.[14]

When the cases are piled up and considered one after the other, we can truly see the results of generations of Legalism. Criminality in the First Emperor's state was a difficult state to escape. Once convicted of a crime, real or imagined, a man would see his income and ranks chipped away until he had nothing left. Nor was there much chance of escaping the cycle: convicts were unable to hold political office, and anyone agreeing to sponsor a convict would be fined themselves.[15]

Confucius might have attracted ridicule with his hopeful notions of kindness to others and human goodness, but in refusing to recognise such a spark of life, Legalism reduced its adherents to animals. Presumably, somewhere in a distant palace, life was not so bad, but for the average inhabitant of Qin, life was a constant round of compulsory government service, timid interactions with neighbours who could turn one in, and constant fear of bucking the status quo. It is perhaps no surprise that one of the First Emperor's greatest modern admirers was Chairman Mao, who imposed similarly restrictive conditions on the populace of China.

Judge Xi's legal documents also contained detailed examinations of crime scene investigations. A discussion of a roadside corpse carefully notes the position and angle of entry wounds, estimating the size and type of the blade that made them. A man was murdered 2,200 years ago within 100 feet of a police post. He was pale, of average height, with shoulder-length black hair. His body was found lying in the road, still clad in his jacket and trousers of low-quality hemp cloth. His shoes were some distance away – he seems to have lost one when running and the other when his assailant caught up with him. Blows had been struck to his chin and temple, but he was killed by a weapon, probably an adze with a 4-inch blade, that struck him once on the neck and twice on the back. On examination of the body, the Qin coroner found two distinguishing marks – old moxibustion scars on the corpse's belly. The body was impounded, the clothes and shoes tagged and logged, and interrogators sent to the local police post to ask if they had noticed anything. An investigator also called on the occupant of a nearby farmhouse to ask if he had heard the sounds of a struggle, or someone calling for help. We do not know how this case ended, but details of its investigation were used as a teaching aid by men like Judge Xi.[16]

The nature of Qin forensics would impress any modern law enforcer, except for the harsh fact that the models are designed not to seek justice, but to assign blame and exact punishments. A Qin investigator is encouraged to look for motive in all deaths, even suicides. If there is no note, he must interrogate friends and relatives in search of a reason; if there is no readily available reason, he is to treat the case as murder and make sure someone pays for it.[17]

The nature of Qin punishments is also the cause of some debate. The severity of a punishment increased in cases of premeditated crime, and was particularly severe if the individual were in a position of responsibility. Officials were fined for losing their seals or documents, and the money would not be returned if the items were later rediscovered. Wardens and thief-catchers in particular were singled out for heavy punitive measures if they abused their position.[18] In one of the more entertaining test cases to be found among Judge Xi's books, two burglars hatch an impromptu plan to co-operate when they meet by chance while both are robbing a house at the same time. When they are caught during their escape, the Qin officials must determine if they have conspired beforehand. If they have, then each is sentenced for the theft of the entire amount; if they have not met before, then each is to be sentenced merely on the basis of the amount he was carrying.[19]

The Qin definition of 'theft' stretched beyond the commission of an act itself. A crime of breaking and entering was considered to have been committed the moment a lock was forced, regardless of whether the criminal actually opened the door. In the eyes of the Qin official, breaking a lock constituted proof of intent to commit burglary, and that itself was punishable by a fine. The interest of Qin officials lay in the smooth running of the Qin state, not in the acquisition of wealth for its citizens. If a man's goat was stolen, he was expected to be grateful for its return, and not to cause a fuss if its leash was missing.

The punishment for perjury or false accusation was the same as that which the perjurer was claiming – falsely accusing someone of murder would lead to one's own execution. Different rules applied to criminals introducing false accusations as part of a plea-bargain. If they were found to be telling lies, they were not executed, but given an extra six years' hard labour.

Since voluntary reporting of others' crimes was such a central part of Qin legal processes, rules were strict on aiding and abetting. In the case of petty crime, leniency was granted to one's neighbours, but an expectation that someone ought to have noticed accompanied increases in the level of a crime. Neighbours were expected to take note of sudden, suspicious increases in wealth, and were steered into reporting it before they shared in it. Such orders even applied to a wife – if her husband suddenly acquired a hundred coins out of nowhere, she could be charged with holding stolen goods if she did not question their origin. If she did so and was told that they were stolen, then she would share the same charge as her husband unless she reported him. Sharing in any way in the profits of the crime would immediately make someone liable to bear the same punishments as the original criminal. In extension of the Qin dynasty's own sternly paternalistic attitude, different rules applied for parents: it was not considered a crime for a father to steal from his children.[20] Slave masters were obliged to sell mothers into slavery along with their children, until such time as the children were able to work for themselves and become less of a burden upon future owners.

The close-knit nature of communities can be seen in the law's demand for sponsors or 'guarantors' for any criminal. A criminal on remand or probation was obliged to provide associates or family members as collateral. If he absconded from his punishment, his sponsors were expected to endure it on his behalf – few criminals would be a flight risk if their actions threatened the lives of several relatives.[21] Bystanders within a hundred paces of any altercation were expected to intervene or face a fine.

Qin legal statutes also contain precise calculations for leniency, based partly on criminal intent but also on the means by which the state might benefit most from the convict's labour. It was a crime to kill a healthy child, but not a crime to kill one that was deformed or disabled. The murder of a law enforcement official was considered to be premeditated, even if the criminal killed in the heat of the moment. Officials who allowed the guilty to go free were subject to serve the same punishment as the man they should have sentenced. It can be seen that in many cases of Qin law, it was best to err on the side of the overly harsh, rather than risk the punishment one might face for being too lenient.[22]

While the punishments applied to all present, any protective elements in the laws only seemed to apply to Qin citizens. Immigrants endured a lower status – if a Qin citizen got into a fight with a foreigner, he would be able to redeem himself with a small payment. Slaves were only partly complicit in the actions of their masters – Qin law acknowledged the difficult line between obedience to one's owner and obedience to law, especially in cases where an unwitting slave was ordered to carry out a relatively blameless act that facilitated a master's crime. Where slaves or citizens were duped by another into criminal acts, such as receiving stolen goods, they were to be let off without charge so long as their innocence could be established.[23]

The currency of many fines was not money, but armour, the better to streamline the process of supplying more material for the ongoing war effort. Since the Qin aristocracy relied too heavily on rewards for military prowess, false claims of achievements in battle were harshly punished, and even officers of rank were partly responsible for their men's performance. Great care was taken with horses, as befits Qin's origins as a pasture. There was a fine for not unharnessing horses after a journey, and the law takes great care to specify where unruly stallions might be located in a team of horses. Sergeants were fined if their crossbowmen were unable to hit a target to an accepted degree of accuracy, and charioteers who could not drive properly would also cause punishment to be passed on to their teachers, and to reimburse the state for the cost of their training.[24]

For learned men who knew the system, there were other ways of manipulating it. During periods of amnesty, Qin officials were instructed to enforce the letter of the First Emperor's decision – it was feasible to steal a thousand coins, spend the profits and get away scot-free, so long as one confessed to the crime during a period of amnesty. However, men who openly abused a position of responsibility were to be sentenced as if they were impostors who had forged their credentials.[25]

In times of particular hardship, Qin citizens might be so bold as to steal food from sacrifices. Qin lawmakers were obliged to come up with statutes defining the values of meat stolen from temple ceremonies. Parts used in a sacrifice were considered more valuable than the leftovers from the sacrificial animal. For as long as a sacrifice was in progress – while the sacred vessels were awaiting the divine presence, or while the temple music continued to play, theft of sacrificial meat was considered to be not only criminal, but also blasphemous. Lesser charges awaited scavengers who lifted castoffs, botched sacrifices and leftovers from waste pits.[26]

Qin penal codes included several grades of execution, of which decapitation was perhaps the most benign. Other crimes required the executioner to cut his victim in half at the waist, or for an individual to be torn apart by four horse-drawn chariots, one

98

attached to each extremity. Some crimes called for a subject to be 'dishonoured' while still alive, presumed to be tattooing, castration or some form of torture, followed by execution. If the convict was a leper, the executioner was spared prolonged contact and permitted to push the victim into water to drown. The fate of a victim's corpse after execution was also a part of the punishment – the more shameful the crime, the greater likelihood that the convict's corpse would be further mutilated, exposed or otherwise dishonoured.

Many sentences contained a combination of the above punishments. The Qin legal statutes make offhand mention of 'palace watchmen', who appear to be convicted criminals so crippled by their punishments that they could only function as glorified door openers. As with other ancient societies with surprisingly high levels of technology, it is often easy to forget that many tasks now carried out by machines were instead carried out by slaves shorn of all vestiges of humanity. The Qin state had no place for the disabled – deformed children were killed at birth, and mutilated adults were expected to work in the 'hidden offices', out of sight of the able-bodied. For the disabled, life in Qin was the epitome of Legalism's desire to turn people into mere cogs in the engine of the state; some of them, quite literally, must have been forced to crouch in alcoves and behind partitions to carry out the most banal functions.[27]

Criminals were readily identifiable by their red clothing – perhaps a snide gesture of disrespect to the fire-themed colours of the preceding Zhou dynasty. Male criminals were also relieved of their beards and, perhaps, eyebrows. Tattooing was a common sentence, although human skin has not been so well preserved over 2,200 years as bronze and terracotta, so it is unclear what a punitive tattoo looked like. Tattooing, however, was regarded as the lightest of the 'mutilations', bodily punishments that extended to include the hacking off of a convict's nose or the removal of one or both feet. The nature of the maiming is thought to be the removal of the toes and front part of the foot, leaving the heel intact – otherwise it is difficult to see how certain mutilated workers would be able to carry out certain hard-labour sentences.

However, where possible, the labour-hungry Qin government preferred its convicts to be sentenced to work details. Some crimes called for total enslavement of the perpetrator, while others set a mandatory period of service. Sentences of hard labour are concealed beneath euphemisms that allude to earlier punishments. Men could be 'sent to gather firewood' for the spirit altars, a series of jobs from chopping wood to stoking palace furnaces. Female convicts were sentenced to 'pound and sift rice'.

Once again, fortune favoured the wealthy or well educated – officials were encouraged not to give menial tasks to skilled artisans or convicts whose abilities could be better used elsewhere. The lightest form of labour punishment was simple bond-service, in which a worker was obliged to perform their occupation without remuneration. At the end of a hard-labour term of service, a convict might hope to have his workload downgraded to wood gathering. For particularly good behaviour, some convicts were able to serve their last couple of years as guards or overseers.

There was one punishment, however, that was regarded as the harshest of all, for which a convict could expect to have his head fully shaven, which was to be sent to the furthest edges of the Qin empire, perhaps never to return, often accompanied by his equally doomed family. It was a back-breaking task that killed many thousands of labourers, who were forced to shovel, hammer and lift in all extremes of weather, from the tearing sands of the desert to the snowy heights of the mountains. On the statute books, this most terrible of sentences could be identified by a single, distinctive word: Wall.

FIVE

The Longest Cemetery

Wall building had long been a regular occupation of ancient Chinese states. Wooden palisades, earth ramparts, ditches or stone walls were used to define borders, although many of them grew out of more agricultural concerns. Qin had its northern and western borders to defend against barbarian influence, but much of the technology of wall building had its origins not in defence, but in farming and communications.

After a Qin army conquered a region, it was soon joined by colonists and workers. Pardoned criminals, undesirables and the disenfranchised were transported to new regions, many of them given the harsh choice between slavery on the new frontier or death back home. All roads, so the saying might have gone, led to Xianyang, fanning out from the Qin capital towards newly conquered regions, mainly to the east, with little road development westwards. This was most obvious in the Sichuan area, one of the first provinces to fall under Qin control, where many decades of public works had forged strong links with the Qin centre. Qin engineers had circumvented the severe mountain regions by constructing a wooden terrace that clung to the mountainside and created a large enough flat area to permit horse-drawn carriages to speed over to Qin's new conquests. A horseman from Xianyang would be able to gallop around perilous mountain passes on wooden terraces, cross rivers on long bridges suspended on lines of boats, and travel some stretches on convoys of linked ships. None of these developments were there for the tourist. As in other empires, they were built to afford swift passage to troops in times of trouble, and to move resources around Qin's conquests. The roads and canals south to Sichuan linked the Qin capital to one of China's richest area for iron- and salt-mining, north they afforded passage to the horse plains that supplied Qin's beasts of burden, and east to the conquered nations of China proper.

From the earliest times, state organisation in China had been largely based on water monopolies – the need to tame the unpredictable rivers, many of which had wide or non-existent flood plains. This became increasingly important in the centuries preceding the First Emperor as the ancient states embraced rice agriculture. From 1000 BC onwards, the ancient Chinese con- structed ever-greater numbers of rice paddies, a process that involved levelling the ground, pounding the porous undersoil until it would not drain dry, and then walling in each field with a barrier and drainage ditch. It was back-breaking labour, but it also multi- plied food resources by a factor of ten, and turned every peasant in the eastern world into someone with basic knowledge of wall construction and irrigation.[1]

One of the main achievements of the states of pre-Qin China lay in their successful construction of dams and levees to control local water supplies. Such projects were also a large source of local tension, since they required workers obtained through compulsory corvée service, or suitable numbers of slaves and captured soldiers from rival nations. The dam schemes were also notoriously parochial, since state borders often followed natural features. A mountain was a difficult object to move, but a river was unpredictable. There are many cases in early Chinese history of a state protecting itself from flood by unleashing ruinous torrents onto a neighbour. The danger of such unnatural disasters made the construction of water defences a vital part of ancient Chinese statecraft – many of the 'walls' that marked state borders did not begin as walls at all, but dikes designed to steer floodwaters.[2]

As the states jostled for supremacy, wall building took on a new character. In the four centuries before the ascendancy of the First Emperor, the states had put their criminals, war captives and dispossessed to work. Chu, Land of the Immaculate, had been the first, and the others followed suit. Qi, Land of the Devout, marked its border with a network of short walls linking river defences to impassable cliffs. The scheme strengthened the land of Qi so much that it conquered other neighbouring regions, forcing it to redraw its borders and build new walls. There was not one 'great wall' in China, but a thousand, forming a network of largely redundant barriers, each a fading memory of a time when a border or river once stood somewhere nearby. With the ascendancy of the First Emperor, almost all of the walls became superfluous to requirements. Those that still had some water control function were maintained, while others were left to fall into ruin. Those few that were of stone construction were often broken up over the years by local builders in search of ready-made bricks.

Now that China had been forcibly unified by the First Emperor, the interior walls were no longer required, but there was still a national border that needed to be defended. To the east, the First Emperor's domain ended at the sea. To the south and west, the mountains of the Tibetan plateau and the jungles of Indochina formed a strong enough barrier to prevent any concern among the Qin administrators. However, to the north and west, modern Mongolia and Siberia, there remained the constant threat of barbarians.

The Qin walls only protected Qin, but now that Qin was responsible for the entire frontier, the First Emperor put managers to work on one of his most famous projects, the linking of the Qin wall with that which protected the northern frontier of Zhao, Land of Latecoming, and Yan, Land of Swallows.

Such a project was a massive undertaking, but there was man-power to spare. The northern wall region was the final frontier for the Qin, separated into twelve marches. Each region was a military zone, maintained largely for the supply of the wall-building garrisons. Its easternmost point was legendary *Shanhai*, the Pass on the Sea, where the mountains dropped suddenly to leave a narrow corridor of flat ground. There, the wall was extended out into the sea itself, and above the gate to the north a sign simply read: 'First Pass under Heaven'. Southwards, to the Chinese mind, lay the World. North lay nothing but forests and mountains.[3] However, the

Shanhai Pass was not the location of the Qin wall, but of later defences. The Qin wall was far to the north of Shanhai, protecting the Liaodong Peninsula in addition.

Meng Tian, son of the family of generals and a trusted servant of the First Emperor, was placed in charge of the wall project. The grand plan was to construct a road across the Ordos Plateau, affording easy passage to the upper reaches of the Yellow River. In doing so, the Qin state would expand its borders over the home pastures of several barbarian tribes – known collectively to the Chinese as the *Hu*. The Great Wall, cutting off the approaches just north of the river, would ensure that the Qin heartland was further protected.

There was nothing particularly new about Meng Tian's project. In fact, his road scheme reached north from the previous Qin wall, which encompassed the former regions of the Rong and Di barbarians, and may have even included some of their own walls, designed to keep out the people of *Qin*.[4] What made a real difference was the sheer scale.

Although the road scheme was never fully completed, and the location of parts of the Great Wall are only matters of modern conjecture, Meng Tian's project was a vast undertaking. It formed a territorial marker, but also a fortress, both for further expansion north and for the administration of the area immediately to the south. Archaeology along its ruins has determined that the local 'barbarians' were not ousted in favour of colonists, but often permitted to live among them. Many of them were also only 'barbarians' through the misfortune of not being from Qin – like the forgotten people of ancient Sichuan, they came from civilised, long-standing cultures, wiped out and wiped over by the onslaught of the Qin armies. Wall building was thus an impressive undertaking, an endeavour of temporary military occupation which gave way to the slower progress of the thousands of workers.

The wall utilised natural features where possible, running along ridges for extra height; almost half the Qin wall was situated at the top of a slope, with the north side dug away to create a sheer barrier. Where the terrain was naturally treacherous, the wall occasionally petered out completely. A fifth of its span contains no 'wall' at all, but instead strongpoints and forts blocking the narrow entrance to otherwise impassable valleys.

But where the Great Wall genuinely *was* a wall, earth to make it was provided from a ditch dug in front, creating an extra obstacle for any would-be attacker. Its construction was largely of layer upon layer of rammed earth, following the same building practices as the lesser walls throughout the south, and on a much smaller scale, the basic construction of any rice paddy. However, in places where additional strength was needed, close to rivers or on low floodplains, the wall's construction materials included rocks and stones in order to add longevity. Where soldiers were stationed for a particularly long time, or stronger defences were thought necessary, the construction of the wall involved more stone than earth. Today, such locations are best preserved far from civilisation. Too close to later human habitation, and the stone portions were broken up for building by later generations. Additional mounds still extant at intervals along the wall suggest that there were also raised platforms forming watch or signal towers.

There is much research still to be done on the nature of the wall, particularly since centuries of later additions and improvements have made it difficult to tell where the Qin wall was. Popular modern images of the Great Wall are actually of the Ming wall, built many centuries after the First Emperor's efforts. Where the Ming wall occupies the same ground as its Qin predecessor, it has usually wiped away all traces of it.

Parts of the Qin wall may not have been completed, but others may have faded away with time. We know that the First Emperor travelled to supervise the construction in his later years, so presumably the first stage of the accompanying road building was completed. Archaeologists have found the start and end of Meng Tian's road to the capital, but the middle is lost under the Ordos, presumed eroded along with the wall that may have run alongside.

In other areas, parts of the wall may have been carried away by 2,000 years of erosion, while other apparent 'gaps' may indicate areas where an earlier defensive feature – a wooden platform perhaps, or a river – no longer exists.

For the workers, it was a tough job, but also seems to have been a matter of pride. The Qin legal statutes decreed that only former workers could be put in charge of work-gangs. Officials were forbidden from putting anyone in charge of a wall-building platoon who had not lifted rocks himself, but whether this is to save the labourers from overwork or the superviser from attack is not clear. At least, according to the records, the workers did not go hungry; while the toil may have been arduous and dangerous, wall-builders were relatively well fed; the successful Qin dynasty irrigation projects, themselves often constructed with slave labour, had seen to that.[5]

The early twentieth-century traveller William Geil collected many folktales during his walk along the length of the Great Wall. In one village alone, among locals so backward that the sight of a photograph noticeably spooked them, Geil heard that the wall was constructed by Ying Zheng himself, riding a magical horse borne on the clouds. Three times in each Chinese league, Ying Zheng stamped his foot, causing a tower to spring up.

Tall tales have rules of their own. Pick an inexplicable phenomenon and stories of gods and demons soon follow. But other elements of the Geil accounts seem to contain references to long-forgotten truths. When the peasants of the Chinese interior talk of the First Emperor 'stamping his feet', are they repeating their ancestors' tales of the way the rammed-earth wall was constructed? Other folktales claim that there were eighteen suns in the sky while the wall was built, perhaps a reference to the never-ending shift work. Men, says the Geil account, 'worked so long that grass had time to grow in the dust which lodged in their heads', perhaps an oblique reference to the arrival of shaven convicts who soon gained stubble.

One of the most telling elements of the Chinese folk stories is the sheer disbelief occasioned by the wall. Geil's interviewees spoke of magic because they could not comprehend the organisational alternative. They speak of the First Emperor having a giant shovel that could fling up an entire stretch of wall in a day – a preposterous story, but one that may contain a dim memory of the speed with which so many thousands of workers could accomplish their tasks. But for those who huddled in the shadow of the wall two millennia after its construction, the simplest explanation lay in tales that bore an uncanny resemblance to the ancient stories of a golden age. To Geil's interviewees, a venture like the wall was simply a modern impossibility – the ancients had only managed it because they were 12 feet tall, not puny like modern men. Another version of the same story adds the evidence of bones 'four feet long' – did elephants form an unrecorded component among the builders, or did the locals simply stumble upon dinosaur fossils?[6]

Similar confusions may have informed another tale, in which the Qin policy of manacling enslaved wall-builders appears to have transformed into another magical story. An unnamed deity supposedly took pity on the cruel tyranny of the First Emperor and sent down a magical thread from heaven that bound the workers together. The thread gave them combined strength, such that the emperor was inspired to use it to make a whip, which only encouraged the workers to still greater achievements.

An oft-repeated folktale, even in modern China, claims that Meng Tian's idle days of wall-building supervision led to an important discovery. Inspired by the daily sight of the lashed workers, or driven to experimentation by many inactive hours spent sitting in a tent and swatting flies, Meng Tian had an idea. Instead of scratching his communiqués to Xianyang on strips of bamboo, he *painted* them. His early prototypes may have involved a piece of wood terminating in a leather flap; later on, he hit upon something that seemed based on a fly swat, its business end comprising a clump of animal hair. When dipped into a pot of ink, the tuft of hair would retain enough of it to permit the wielder to daub a character on a suitable surface, and not only the traditional bamboo strip or wooden slat. The invention of paper was still centuries away, but the use of this new device would permit writing on silk. Meng Tian, so the legend goes, had invented the writing brush.

Just as it linked earlier fortifications, the magnitude of the Wall drew older legends to it. One tale, about Meng Jiang-nü, the anguished widow of a wall-builder, is now associated with the Qin wall, even though it was first recorded centuries earlier. According to the original, a wife made a long journey to a wall between Qi and Lü, long before the time of the Qin emperor. When she discovered that her husband had died during his hard-labour sentence, her desolate scream caused a section of a city's walls to crumble. After the building of the Great Wall, the tale was relocated, its characters renamed, until by the Tang dynasty it was the tale of a faithful wife bringing winter clothes to her husband in one of Meng Tian's work parties. The tragic woman was memorialised in plays and poetry, and even had temples built in her honour.

As time passed and sections of the wall were more likely to be found in disrepair, the opportunities to discuss mythical reasons for it only grew. By the twentieth century, the tale had taken on still more folkloric aspects. Some in the Chinese hinterland now claimed that the Great Wall had originally encircled China completely, but that the widow's screams had destroyed an entirely legendary southern section, presumed to reach from the mouth of the Yangtze all the way to Tibet. In another variant found at a different part of the wall's course, the widow's screams brought down the wall for a reason: to expose the corpses of the men buried inside. Biting her finger, she walked among the bodies until her falling blood landed on a corpse that moved, thereby identifying her loving husband in order to arrange for his proper burial.[7]

The predictably high number of deaths among the slave labourers led to other stories, seemingly inspired by accounts of the burying of bodies within the wall. The most famous capitalises on the First Emperor's reputation for strange superstitions, claiming that a soothsayer advised him the wall would never be completed until 10,000 men had been buried within it. Supposedly, such a prophecy was too much even for the heartless Ying Zheng, although he was able to find a compromise that was lucky for almost everyone. He sent his men to screen the workers until they found a man called *Wan*, 'ten thousand', and buried him inside the wall instead.

Tales of men walled up beneath the fortifications, coupled with later views of collapsed cross-sections, inspired later generations to suggest that the wall contained hidden rooms full of buried treasure. In a tale that may bear an indirect relation to that of Aladdin in the *Arabian Nights*, the peasants of Central Asia described a tramp in ancient times who gained access to one of the First Emperor's treasure hoards through a secret door. However, he was trapped inside the room until he dropped all the gold and jewels he was carrying, after which the gods supposedly emptied the chamber to prevent anyone else gaining access.[8]

Not all of the wall-workers were men. One of the many criminal sentences for women of the Qin era was that of 'rice-pounder', originally assumed by translators to mean the preparation of food or milling of grains. However, the sentence may not have referred to agricultural hard labour, but to a posting in the wall zone, chained in a line, tamping endless buckets of rice into paste for use in the making of wall cement.[9]

Later generations were unable to reproduce the incredible hardness and sticking power of the wall's mortar, and claimed that it had magical properties. Lumps of it were prised from ruins of the wall and ground into powder by alchemists, who claimed it would heal wounds. One of Geil's twentieth-century folklore sources repeated a formula for treating cuts and burns, using a salve made of equal parts ground wall mortar and mouse embryo. A speck of wall mortar the size of a lotus seed could also be taken internally as a cure for stomach ache.[10]

The combination of many earlier fortifications also led to many apparent dead ends in the Great Wall, particularly in later centuries where an abutment that once ran into a river might be left high and dry. Local folklore even supplied an explanation for that, discounting the extreme organisation of the historical wall in favour of a haphazard scheme, claiming that the wall-builders were forced to mark their foundations in the trail left by the dragged saddle of the First Emperor's horse. This, supposedly, was the random origin of some of the Great Wall's stranger choices of direction.

Other tales similarly invert cause and effect. One original aim of the Qin wall was undoubtedly to keep out the northern nomads, but also to mark the edge of Qin territory. Later generations in central China, witnessing the harsh desert to the north, would claim that the wall functioned as a barrier to *feng shui*, and that the reason for the desert was that civilisation was blocked from advancing further. The Great Wall even lent its mystique to places far away. Chinese legend held that the savage races of the hinterland owed their small stature and rough existence to their origins as workers who had fled the wall to eke out a meagre existence in the deserts and mountains.[11]

The construction of the Great Wall took many years, and would occupy servants of the First Emperor for the rest of his life. But he took an interest in it from the earliest days of its construction. Only a few months after the last of the rival states had fallen, the First Emperor left Xianyang to see the wall zone for himself.

It was in 220 that the First Emperor and his entourage made the first of several inspection trips, heading west up the Wei River into the highlands. His journey took him up past the former capitals of Qin when it had been nothing but a military outpost, and up beyond the source of the Wei River itself to the place where his great-grandfather, the Bright King, had constructed an earlier wall to mark Qin's eastern frontiers.

At Long-xi, the First Emperor could stand on the rammed earth rampart and gaze towards the west, secure in the knowledge that his domain was safe. The First Emperor then travelled west along the old wall, before turning back down one of the Wei tributaries to the fort of Beidi, and after a brief detour to Mount Jidou, presumably for an unrecorded ceremony, he passed back through the town of Huizhong and to his capital once more. Although the journey barely described the borders of ancestral Qin, it was still several hundred miles, and appears to have proved somewhat more arduous than expected. On his return, the First Emperor ordered the construction of better roads, and, to show that he was not all bad, advanced everyone in his empire by one rank.[12]

Having seen the wastes of his empire's far east, the First Emperor announced that his next inspection tour would be considerably farther ranging, taking in the eastern shores where his domain fell into the limitless ocean. On the way, he would visit the gods themselves, and let them know that he was the ruler of the world.

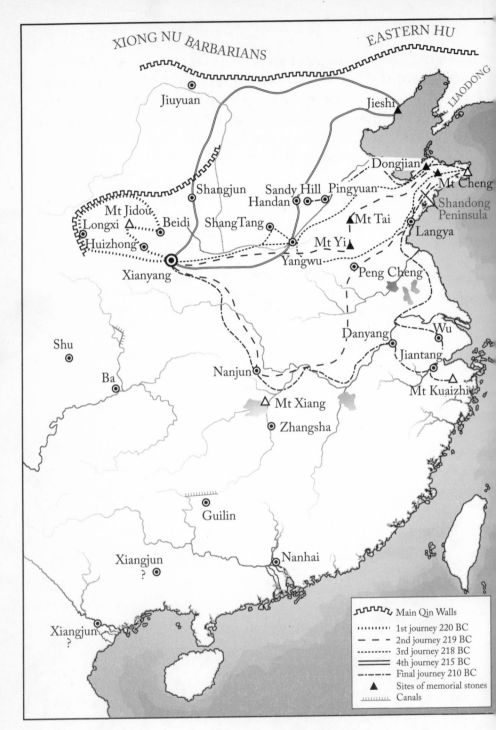

The journeys of the First Emperor.

SIX

The Burning of the Books

The place of pilgrimage for the kings of old was supposedly Mount Tai, the tall peak that sat on the borders of the old homeland of the great sage Confucius, now firmly within the realm of the First Emperor. Although the Qin dynasty had already ridden roughshod over many traditions, the First Emperor seemed keen to order a trip to Mount Tai. Getting there would utilise the new imperial roads, and also permit him to examine some of the outlying regions of his empire for the first time – while the First Emperor is renowned as the conqueror of China, much of the conquering was actually done by others.

En route, the First Emperor's party left a memorial stone at Mount Yi, outlining their successes. Later legends would arise concerning the stone, claiming that its carving was personally supervised by Li Si, and hence the most perfect version of his approved 'small script' calligraphy. The site became a place of constant pilgrimage for later generations of scholars, all hoping to take a rubbing from the monument to aid their own presentation. The locals became so incensed at the constant arrivals of tourists that they eventually destroyed part of the monument with fire. This proved to be of little use in deterring tourists who, so claimed a Tang dynasty almanac, 'kept coming like arrows'. Eventually, a copy was made and set up in the prefectural office for public consultation, thereby allowing the villagers to get on with their lives undisturbed.[1]

The stone memorial was the first of many attempts by the Qin administration to make its presence felt in the empire, but the journey to Mount Tai was the most important. Traditionally, new rulers were supposed to construct an altar terrace on the summit, where they would make their devotions to heaven, before journeying back down the mountainside to a small hillock near its base, where they would offer similar prayers to the earth. However, the nature of such ceremonies was beyond the martial people of Qin, causing the First Emperor to send for local scholars to advise him.

Here, perhaps, we see the first intimations of a deeper insecurity, almost a sense of class anxiety. Confucius and other scholars of old had left many detailed instructions on the correct way to maintain the Mandate of Heaven, but the Qin dynasty had been too busy fighting wars to pay much attention. Even the learned men in the First Emperor's entourage were at a loss – practical matters were fine, but getting the ceremonies exactly right required advice from outsiders.

Even so, the First Emperor was not really listening. After consulting with several dozen Confucians in the Mount Tai region, his advisers informed him that Mount Tai was wholly sacred, such that not even the ancient kings would dare to harm it. Instead, they would wrap the wheels of their carriages in cattail leaves so that their progress along the mountain road would be softer and less liable to leave tracks or ruts, or damage the plants.

Initially, the First Emperor complied, only to sit impatiently in his carriage as it lumbered with increased slowness on its padded wheels. In what appears to have been a track too hazardous for horses, the First Emperor's carriage was pulled by his own followers, who found it hard going when much of the traction had been compromised by, of all things, leaves.

Eventually, the First Emperor tired of the charade, and announced that since men without number had perished before his armies, he was not about to admit defeat to trees and grass. He ordered the wheels unwrapped and for attendants to march ahead with knives, hacking a path through the undergrowth.

At the summit, he performed the required ceremonies with due solemnity, only to be interrupted by a storm. As the wind rose up and dark clouds threatened a downpour, attendants began to wonder if it were a sign. The First Emperor's decrees made it plain over and over again that he was the rightful ruler of the world, chosen by the gods, and yet they elected to ruin his big ceremony with bad weather. One could not simply ignore bad omens while reiterating the good, there were far too many witnesses for that. Whether the First Emperor was superstitious or not, he was obliged to at least pretend to be.

As the rain began pouring, the First Emperor was forced to curtail his ceremony and dash for cover, huddling in his wet robes underneath a pine tree. While thunder rattled around the mountaintop, the First Emperor reportedly asked the tree for mercy. Some time later, in honour of the occasion, he conferred the rank of Junior Grand Master on it.[2]

Bedraggled and somewhat cowed, the imperial party made its way back down the mountainside to Liangfu Hill to perform the companion ceremony to the earth. There, according to the *Record of the Historian*, they also erected a stone tablet that showed the emperor's achievements for all to see:

The First Emperor is ordained, decrees made, laws elucidated, heeded by his loyal subjects. In the 26th year [of his reign], all under heaven is united, all obey his word. He cares for the Black Headed People in distant corners; he ascends Mount Tai and views the eastern end. His obedient subjects mark his deeds from their very beginning, and celebrate his virtues. His politics progress, all things find their place, all have laws to define them. Great and manifest, his quality transcends the generations, to be borne without alteration. The holy Emperor, pacifier of all under heaven, reigns without tiring. He rises early, retires late, makes plans that long bring benefits, and offers wise counsel. His teachings spread to the distance, near and far find order according to his will. High and low are separated and clarified, men and women behave accordingly, each to their allotted roles. His glory permeates within and without, [so that] everywhere there is peace and quiet, which will extend to prosperity. May his influence reach to infinity, all receive and follow this testament, and ever accept these solemn precepts.[3]

After the ceremonies at Mount Tai, the First Emperor's entourage headed further along the northern coast of Shandong to the easternmost point of his empire. The First Emperor's progress then continued back along the southern coast of Shandong before heading inland again at the picturesque Mount Langya. The site was famed for its scenery, and had been chosen by an ancient king as the ideal place to build a tower overlooking the sea. But the Langya tower was now in ruins, causing the First Emperor to announce that he would have it rebuilt, and at a suitably more ostentatious level than the original, since he was an emperor and the original builder had been a mere king. However, the First Emperor caused some consternation among his subjects by announcing that he would remain at Langya to observe the renovations. He had, after all, seen the massive ramparts of the western wall and the impressive achievements in road building and architecture throughout his domain. Langya Tower would be a similarly impressive monument, and, to what must have been his followers' intense annoyance, the emperor was going to stay and watch. He was sure, he said, it would only take a few weeks.[4]

Despite the efforts of the work teams, and the conscription of thousands of peasants from the surrounding area to drag rocks along the slopes, the project took several months. Local legend holds that a number of bitter folk songs date back to the project, lamenting farmers' fates, torn away from their fields to labour on a pointless imperial folly, starving while their crops rotted unharvested. Eventually, the tower was complete, and the elated emperor arranged for another memorial to be carved into a monument, which praised, without a scrap of irony, the wondrous way his imperial grace brought happiness to his people.

Although not mentioned in the *Record of the Historian*, we can hazard a reasonable guess at what happened next. The First Emperor had already looked out over the seas to the east at the empire's furthermost point. Now, at Langya, he had one last opportunity to do so, and mused aloud about what may lie beyond the horizon. The *Record of the Historian* picks up the story at Langya, with the arrival of men who could supply an answer.

Something had happened to the First Emperor during his journey to Shandong. Perhaps it was the weight of his achievements and responsibilities. Apart from a childhood in Handan, the Historian makes no record of the First Emperor physically experiencing the world beyond Qin until after his coronation. Perhaps it was only after undertaking a journey of many hundreds of miles that he was beginning to appreciate what had been done in his name. Now, he had seen its furthest frontiers, and witnessed for himself just what could be achieved through the harsh application of the Qin laws.

Although born to a dynasty that scorned superstition, and educated by a man whose disdain for the supernatural was legendary, the First Emperor had begun to worry about his own mortality.

Perhaps the emperor had been led into such thoughts by the elaborate preparations for his royal tomb. The commission of an imperial mausoleum would have, however nobly, drawn attention to the fact that the First Emperor, while revered as the embodiment of perfection, would inevitably die. After gaining the world, the First Emperor was forced to recognise that he would eventually leave it behind.

The First Emperor refused to believe it. It is not uncommon for accounts of royalty to allude to insanity – what could be more insane than being set up as a living god, reared for imperial excellence and appointment as the earthly representative of an unknowable divine order? As he entered his forties, his mid-life crisis manifested itself in extreme ambition. He had already done the impossible by conquering the world, so how hard would it be to conquer death?

Thanks to the onerous responsibilities of organising a suitable ritual on Mount Tai, the imperial entourage had gained a following of local wise men. Some were learned men who had spent their lives studying the Confucian classics and debating fine points of court protocol. Some were charlatans.

One of the latter group was Xufu, a man from the Land of the Devout who claimed to know Taoist secrets of immortality. There was a magic pill, he claimed, that could make a man live forever. He informed the First Emperor that there was indeed something beyond

117

the eastern seas. Some days' sail away, there was a chain of three holy islands where the immortals themselves could be found. Suddenly, the First Emperor was interested. He pressed the self-professed sorcerer, and perhaps Xufu realised that he was digging his own grave. In what may have been an attempt to fudge the issue, Xufu assured the emperor that it was very difficult, almost impossible, for human beings to approach the isles of the immortals. Only qualified wizards and pure youths and maidens might be able to approach.

It sounded like a good enough risk to the First Emperor, who immediately authorised the commission of a fleet, to be crewed by Xufu and his cronies, with a thousand virgin boys and girls to be rounded up from the region. The First Emperor wanted Xufu to go in search of the isles of the immortals, to find the miracle immortality pills and bring some back for his ruler.[5]

Xufu's exploration venture was not the only hare-brained scheme authorised by the First Emperor. As the entourage made its way back west from the coast, leaving Xufu somehow to draft his virgin crews, the First Emperor stopped in at Peng-cheng. There he continued with prayers and sacrifices, intent on locating an important artefact. He had seen the western walls of his great-grandfather the Bright King. He had seen the eastern ocean, the existence of which he had previously only taken on faith. He believed that loyal sorcerers were going in search of the potion that would make him live forever, so perhaps it is not surprising that he was more susceptible to other beliefs.

He also ordered the construction of further monuments to his greatness, for which he, or his stone-carvers, among the usual statements of imperial glory and lasting wondrousness, saw fit to make a comparison between the First Emperor and the sovereigns of legend. It was a sign of increasing hubris, since the First Emperor, or his stone-carvers, regarded his achievement as somehow greater than that of the demi-gods of old. In his estimation, he had conquered an area even larger than that defined as the 'under heaven' of Chinese myths. Moreover, thanks to the Legalist system pioneered by Lord Shang, instituted over many decades in Qin and brought to fruition by Lü Buwei and Li Si, the First Emperor believed that his government was better, too. His inscription said, of the ancient sovereigns:

> The Sovereigns of ancient times had knowledge that was disordered, and laws that were disunified. They posed as divine beings to deceive and frighten their different subjects, but their deeds did not live up to their boasts, and so their reigns did not endure. Even before their deaths, their nobles rebelled, and their laws went unheeded.[6]

The implication was clear – the great men of the past, so revered by previous generations, were nothing compared to the First Emperor. But even as the empire promulgated its old-style Qin disdain of religion, its ruler continued to drift ever further into superstition.

Peng-cheng was the legendary site of one of his great-grandfather's setbacks. During the Bright King's grab for power and battles with the doomed Zhou dynasty, he had attempted to gain the powerful magical artefacts known as the Nine Tripods. But one had eluded him and allegedly 'flown away' from the Royal Domain. If one believed in the Ninth Tripod, and clearly someone in the First Emperor's entourage was giving it enough credence, then it may have been the vital missing factor that prevented the Bright King from becoming the ruler of the world long before his great-grandson. By that token, the First Emperor owed it to his ancestor to locate the missing artefact, and owed it to his dynasty's future success to secure it for himself. The Ninth Tripod, according to the Qin state's record, had flown through the air far to the east, where it had crash-landed somewhere suitably distant to be of nothing but academic concern to the Qin chroniclers. Sure in the knowledge that nobody would be able to go and look, they estimated its last known resting place in the Land of the Devout, in a river near Peng-cheng.[7]

At the time, the Land of the Devout had been the most powerful rival state, but also the most distant. In later generations, the rival's supposed possession of the Ninth Tripod had presented a handy excuse for the coalition forces that toppled the one regime that could have contended with Qin for mastery of all under heaven. But now that there was a First Emperor, he wanted the Ninth Tripod for himself, and he was prepared to wait while a thousand divers searched the river. The *Record of the Historian* does not say how long he idled on the banks, but he seems to have lost patience relatively quickly. Assuming that the artefact would soon be found, the entourage left the divers to it and moved on, heading further to the south.

A later folktale, recorded in Li Daoyuan's *Commentary on the River Classic* of the northern Wei dynasty, seems to refer to the sighting, or presumed sighting, of the Ninth Tripod. Supposedly, the First Emperor was told that the Ninth Tripod had been seen in the river. But although the dredgers' rope caught on something below the surface 'when they tried to pull the tripod out, a dragon bit the rope in two. Therefore the local people whispered, "No sooner did it bring delight, than the line of the tripod was cut."'[8]

It was a bad omen for the First Emperor, since the 'line of the tripod', as written in Chinese, could refer to either a rope around a cauldron or a dynasty hoping to achieve absolute power – if thwarted in one meaning, it was implied, Ying Zheng would be defeated in both.

The First Emperor intended to take in all four corners of his domain. Although his armies would press further to the south in his own lifetime, the southernmost point he reached in his own travels was Mount Xiang on what had formerly been the southern marches of Chu, Land of the Immaculate. According to legend, Mount Xiang was the burial site of the Princesses Ehuang and Nüying, daughters of a divine ruler of legend, who had also become the concubines of his nominated successor. The bamboo groves on the mountain's slopes were renowned for speckled patterns on the wood, said to be the girls' tears, which fell onto the mountain slopes when they found that their ruler had died from overwork.

Doubtless still smarting from the embarrassments of Mount Tai and the fruitless riverbed search, the First Emperor was in no mood for the bad weather that plagued him on the lake. Seeing the roof of the princesses' shrine in the distance, he angrily asked about its origin. On being told the story of the two princesses, he decreed that they were merely the daughters or bedmates of true greatness and undeserving of their noble titles. Thinking that the spirits of the princesses were responsible for the choppy waters that had almost upended his imperial boat, the First Emperor ordered for the mountain itself to be punished. There was no propitiation for Mount Xiang, instead 3,000 convicts were shipped to the mountain to strip its slopes of all trees and greenery. Another legend of the same event claimed that the First Emperor also ordered the entire mountain to be painted red, the colour of a criminal's clothing, although the *Record of the Historian* restricts itself to reporting the deforestation. It is worth noting that 3,000 Qin convicts swarming all over the mountain in their distinctive scarlet garb would be enough in themselves to 'paint it red'; perhaps this is the origin of the folktale. The shrine itself was set on fire and left to burn as a warning to any other divinities who dared to challenge the First Emperor's power.[9]

The following year, 218, the First Emperor took another journey to the east, revisiting many of the same sites. The plan seems to have been a second visit to Shandong; the easternmost point and the Langya Tower were also on his itinerary, although there does not appear to have been any plan to head south again. The train proceeded with soldiers marching on all sides and thirty-six carriages, many identical, and most flying the traditional black flags of the First Emperor's family and lucky element.

Despite warnings of bandit activity in the region, the First Emperor's entourage continued, only for the peace of its progress to be disrupted by a lump of iron falling from the sky. Somewhere above the train of carriages, a would-be assassin had pushed a heavy weight from a cliff, aiming straight at the carriage he believed to be the First Emperor's. His judgement was out by one, and his assassination anvil instead crushed the carriage directly in front of his actual target, sending debris flying that almost injured the First Emperor.

The assassin did not have quite as lucky an escape. He was apprehended by guards, and taken to Li Si and Zhao Gao for interrogation. He supposedly regaled them with a curse: 'The fatuous and self-indulgent emperor killed the princes and crushed the six states. Won't their descendants kill him? All the loyal officials of the dynasties will have their revenge!'[10]

Refusing to give his name, the man claimed that he had missed deliberately, but then let slip that his only regret was that he had let his young master down. When pressed as to who that mysterious 'young master' might be, he somehow eluded the clutches of his tormentors and killed himself by smashing his head into a nearby column.

The unfortunate demise of the sole suspect did not deter Li Si and Zhao Gao from investigating further. Homing in on the phrases 'young master' and 'loyal officials', they deduced that there was an ideal suspect close by – a man called Ji Ping, whose father had been a chief minister in the state of Han, and who himself had served two kings as an official before the Qin conquest. Ji Ping himself had a young son, angered by the theft of his birthright and with a suitable motive for trying to kill the First Emperor.

Remarkably, Li Si's reasoning was correct. Although many local aristocrats had maintained their lifestyles and former wealth after the Qin conquest, one son of the local Ji family was indeed dissatisfied. He is remembered by posterity as 'Zhang Liang', although that is merely an alias he assumed during his flight from Qin justice. Turning his back on a family rich enough to afford 300 slaves at their mansion, he vowed to avenge the fallen Han rulers, but did so in secret.

Like the earlier plan of the Red Prince, Zhang Liang's operation took a long while in forming. Although he lacked the Red Prince's national budget, he bided his time until a suitable candidate presented himself, the strongman Cang Hai Gong. It was this Cai Hang Gong who was the suicidal would-be assassin, a man who had demonstrated a superhuman ability to throw large weights great distances, although an all-too-human fallibility in the selection of his target. But while the cracked skull of Cang Hai Gong was hacked away from his dead shoulders and put on display on the walls of a local city, Zhang Liang was able to make good his escape. He was forced to spend several years in hiding.[11]

There was a brief and violent display of imperial investigation in the region, designed to ensure that the locals appreciated who was boss. However, it would appear that the incident was covered up to some extent, since the organisers would come forward after the First Emperor's death to reveal that they had escaped with their lives. The imperial party then hastened back to the relative safety of the Langya Tower, which seems to have become something of a coastal retreat for the First Emperor, where he might while away the summer months on the relatively cooler coast, before heading back towards his landlocked capital for winter. Before returning to the Qin heartland, the First Emperor commissioned two further monuments, the text of which makes specific reference to his reforms. If there is any element of truth rather than official spin, by the year 218 the First Emperor believed that Li Si's programmes to unite the laws, weights and measures had been fully implemented.[12]

For the following two years, 217 and 216, as the *Record of the Historian* bluntly puts it, 'nothing happened'. The First Emperor remained in Xianyang and made no further tours out to the coast, perhaps spooked by the latest assassination attempt, or occupied with other tasks. The various building schemes of the wall, other defences, the construction of the public buildings and the massive population movements were probably more than enough to keep a nation busy, and the only decree noted in the annals comes right at the end of 216, when the First Emperor granted an increase in allotted rations to citizens of his empire. However, the reasons for the lack of official activities may have been more personal – the First Emperor may have found a new hobby, one that kept him close to the palace and out of public sight.

After the hardships of unification and consolidation, his 216 decree shows a sign of softening and perhaps satisfaction. China was finally unified, not only in theory, but in practice. However, human nature remained unchanged. It seems that the First Emperor, perhaps bored of palace life, decided to put his own system to the test. Late in 216, he slipped out into the city in disguise accompanied by only four bodyguards.

Outside the palace, nobody knew the First Emperor's face. He was able to walk among his people without fear of assault. Although he set little store by the ancient texts of olden times, it was said that when the great sage Confucius once ran a town along virtuous principles, people began to internalise the laws.[13] People passed each other on the streets with the correct degrees of decorum and respect, lost articles were left where they had fallen so that the owners might find them, and life became harmonious. Perhaps the First Emperor was expecting to find something similar in his capital. Instead, as he wandered along the banks of a city pond, he was jumped by a group of thieves.[14]

His bodyguards, who had presumably been maintaining a discreet distance, soon came to the rescue and swiftly beat the would-be robbers to death. As a result of this attack, the First Emperor returned to his previous severity. After thirty years as the ruler of Qin, and five as the supposed ruler of the world, he had found he was unable to walk outside his own palace without being mugged! Clearly, there was still work to be done.

Considering several other stories about the First Emperor, it is possible that he made many forays out of the palace, but that the Historian only reports the one that almost ended in disaster. It is also conceivable that the attackers were not opportunistic criminals, but assassins who had been informed of his relatively unprotected wanderings by a palace insider. Another folktale about him records an earlier expedition in disguise, in the course of which he listened with rapt attention to gossip about a local man whose great-grandfather had supposedly ridden to heaven on the back of a dragon. The tall tales seem to have convinced the emperor that he was looking in the wrong place for the secret of eternal life. While his various scholarly advisers continued to siphon money out of the imperial coffers in search of alchemical quick fixes, the First Emperor announced that he would seek to follow in the footsteps of the Taoist masters of old. Such figures, it was said, would dwell among the mountains and lakes in simple lives of contemplation, until they divested themselves of earthly concerns and achieved immortality.

The First Emperor determined to try it, but did so with typical brute force. Instead of walking into the wilderness and disappearing, as the ancient Taoist sage Lao Zi had supposedly done, he ordered the construction of a suitable wilderness close to home. A huge pond was dug south of the city, filled with water diverted from the Wei River and surrounded by sculpted rocks and landscaped gardens. Here, the First Emperor spent some time frolicking in his man-made retreat, hoping to achieve some form of Taoist enlightenment. However, when enlightenment and immortality were not swiftly forthcoming, he grew impatient.[15]

Few in the emperor's realm would dare suggest that he was wasting his time, although one man did. He was the First Emperor's court jester, a dwarf whose diminutive size somehow allowed him to get away with outrageously sarcastic comments about his ruler. On hearing of further plans to expand the palace gardens, the jester commented that it would be handy to have so many deer around as an early warning system in case of enemy attack. Although no action was taken at the time, the emperor quietly shelved any expansion scheme in favour of more practical improvements to the city, and gave up his fake life of seclusion.[16]

In 215, he made a fourth inspection tour, heading along the road to his birthplace of Handan before heading north to the former domain of the Red Prince, the Land of Swallows. He left another monument at a place on the coast whose name by the time of the Historian was simply *Jieshi*, 'Stone Tablet', boasting that he had 'exempted the innocent from taxation', and also that he had pulled down city walls in the Land of Swallows. This latter comment may refer to an earlier fortification at the Shanhai Pass, a place where the mountains met the sea on the coastal road to Liaodong. It had in the past and would again at several dates mark the border between China and the 'barbarian' world, but the First Emperor's own border was significantly further north. Pulling down walls at Jieshi would have been a symbolic acceptance that there was no need for them, as they were firmly within the borders of China.[17]

There was another reason for the First Emperor's trip to the north of his kingdom. Supposedly, there was a wise man in what had once been the Land of Swallows who could put him in touch with an immortal. However, this meeting does not seem to have come about, and the First Emperor instructed three of his supernatural 'advisers' to conduct further searches for the elixir of life. Then, his party travelled along the line of Meng Tian's Great Wall, which now linked the northern border of what had been the Land of Swallows to the northern border of what had once been the Land of Latecoming.

Back in the capital there was disappointing news. One of the First Emperor's many supposed 'experts' had returned empty-handed from a long quest in search of the elixir of immortality. However, perhaps in anticipation of imperial anger, he claimed to have received a message from the gods for the First Emperor's ears. It was a simple statement: 'The empire will be destroyed by *Hu*.'

The First Emperor took the message to be a warning that his work was not yet done on the northern border. The Rong and Di barbarians might be incorporated into the empire, but at least two groups defined as *Hu* still remained north of the wall zone. That, at least, was the excuse for a new order to Meng Tian, to conduct a further campaign against the barbarians. Using the newly built wall as a base, Meng Tian sallied forth with tens of thousands of men, advancing far into Inner Mongolia before returning to report suitable pacification once more.[18]

The northern border was not the only place where the First Emperor ordered a clean-up. Similarly sweeping reforms were made to the criminal justice system, particularly regarding tax-dodgers. Qin taxation was levied on the head of each household, which had created a technical loophole that would exclude a man from taxation if, instead of setting up his own household upon reaching his majority, he took his wife's name and sought adoption into her family. The practice, common throughout Chinese history, was designed to ensure that, in cases where a family lacked a male heir, the family name would be continued through the adoptive son-in-law, thus ensuring that there would always be a descendant to carry out the necessary rituals of ancestor worship. However, it would appear that far too many of the First Emperor's subjects were bending the letter of the law and signing up as adoptees simply to save money. Considering the Qin dynasty's historical disdain for religion, and the First Emperor's increasing frustration with his search for magic aids that actually worked, his reaction was predictable. In 214, the First Emperor ordered that all such tax-dodgers, along with a number of fugitives from justice, convicts and other undesirables, should be rounded up and packed off to the far south, where they would serve on a new frontier.

An army of the Qin empire pushed further south than Chinese had ever been before, following a tributary of the Yangtze River to its south-western extreme, and then traversing the mountain range into the basin beyond. The expedition established three new commanderies in the south, Guilin, Xiangjun and Nanhai. Although the exact locations are still open to conjecture, it is thought that *Guilin*, 'Cassia Woods', was roughly equivalent to the place that bears that name today, while *Nanhai*, 'South-Sea', was somewhere near modern Canton. *Xiangjun*, 'Elephant-District', is more problematic and may have been somewhere near modern Kunming, or perhaps even further to the south, where the Red River meets the Gulf of Tonkin. The region as a whole was designated as the place of the 'Southern Yue' peoples, *Nan-yue* (locally *Nam-viet*), using the same characters that are now transposed and pronounced Vietnam.

The expansion to Nan-yue moved the First Emperor's borders all the way to another sea coast in the south-east, and seemingly impassable jungles and mountains in the south-west. Now, finally, he might consider his job of conquering the world finally accomplished, at least geographically. Some of his subjects, however, were still not playing by the draconian rules of Legalism. For so many men to have successfully avoided taxation or justice, there had to be a large number of law enforcers and judges who were not fulfilling their duties. Consequently, the year 213 saw a purge of all officials thought to have failed in their responsibilities. They were packed off to join the criminals they had once sentenced, either on further Great Wall labours in the north or hacking out a colony on the new southern frontier.

It was widely agreed that there was finally cause for celebration. With the great Legalist plan finally believed to be a success, the First

Emperor gave a huge banquet at his palace in Xianyang. It was attended by the eldest of his children, lords and officials of note, and a group of his most trusted political advisers, known as the Seventy Erudites.

As the banquet reached its climax, one of the officers proposed a toast. Years of imperial service had taught him the best policy to follow, and his speech was a textbook glorification of the First Emperor suitable for one of the stone tablets dotted all over the empire. The First Emperor, he said, was truly great, he had accomplished many things, allowing the territory of Qin to expand beyond its borders, seizing control of formerly independent states, and even places far beyond. Moreover, in his implementation of new laws and pacification measures, the First Emperor had created a new state that would endure for the rest of time.

The toastmaster finished with a flourish, and when the First Emperor acknowledged his praise, the banqueting hall erupted with cheers and applause. But not all the diners were pleased with his version of events, and one scholar from the district that had once been the Land of the Devout took drunken exception. His name was Chun Yuyue, and he spoke the secret concerns of a number of the First Emperor's scholars, and possibly a few of the First Emperor's children. Emboldened by alcohol, he flew in the face of Qin policy by recalling olden times, pointing out that it had been a policy in the days of the legendary sovereigns to parcel out marches and fiefdoms to those who had served them faithfully, and indeed to family members. If Chun Yuyue's complaint was anything to go by, numerous officials in the Qin war machine had failed to appreciate all the clauses in the Legalist agenda, and had served in the expectation of being granted small kingdoms of their own upon the completion of the Qin conquest. However, Li Si's Legalist system was far more flexible than that. As part of his policy of keeping control centralised, no official was safe. Instead, uneasy triumvirates and temporary contracts governed many provincial regions, and the First Emperor maintained the right to depose or replace any of his 'nobles' at short notice. The implications of this policy were increasingly unwelcome to the First Emperor's sons, possibly a dozen boys of whom perhaps only one, Prince Fusu, stood a chance of attaining political power, and even then only with his father's approval.

But if he spoke with the silent support of the princes, Chun Yuyue gave no sign. He limited his speech to a complaint about the Qin empire's wilful ignorance of tradition. Chun Yuyue was a follower of the Confucian school, and hence believed that many traditions existed for a reason. Chun thought that the First Emperor's system of prefectures and counties was not benign at all, but an unstable danger, particularly since anyone who really deserved to be given control of a province would disqualify themselves through their own loyalty.

Chun Yuyue's comments were not popular, but he spoke well enough to gain the First Emperor's attention. He asked his closest adviser to respond, perhaps an unwise choice of speaker, since Li Si was personally responsible for the organisation of the prefecture system, and likely to have taken the criticism as a personal attack. Li Si admitted that the system still had teething troubles, but in the half-dozen years since it was first instituted, it seemed to be working.

We will never know if Li Si's next comments were made in the heat of the moment, or if he merely chose to suggest a policy he had been mulling over for some time. Certainly his past activities, particularly in the reform of the writing system and government institutions, had set him on a road that made his next suggestion wholly characteristic. After brushing off Chun Yuyue's comments with disdain, Li Si pointed out to the First Emperor that such ignorant carping was likely to continue for some time in the future. The Legalist system that had so successfully conquered the world was new, argued Li Si. It was the product of the Qin empire, and so far it had proved to be the best system that the world had ever seen.

Chun Yuyue had made a fatal error in appealing to ancient precedents. In criticising Li Si, he had also gone up against one of the foremost minds of the age. Li Si toyed with his prey and remarkably found a way of demolishing the argument, both with recourse to Chun Yuyue's own philosophical system and that of Legalism itself.

Li Si pointed out that Chun Yuyue's argument was based on a false premise. He was appealing to some nebulous idea of ancient perfection, although it was well known that the ancients were not perfect. The several mythical kings had each pursued different policies and systems, and all their policies had been found wanting. Li Si was able to use the very question that had first led to the formation of the Legalist system, *If the ancient kings were so perfect, then what had gone wrong?* It had taken one truly great king, the man who became the First Emperor, to prove what the Legalists had always suspected, that the ancient legends were lies.

Of course, this was unfair. Chun Yuyue had a point, that the Zhou dynasty preceding Qin had lasted for almost a thousand years, and that Qin had been barely in control for a decade. Li Si was being grossly overconfident in his assessment of the Qin dynasty's achievement, but there seemed to be no way of saying so without angering the emperor.

The impasse was precisely the kind of protocol issue that Li Si's late rival Han Fei had discussed at length in his *Frustrations of a Loner*, which the First Emperor had once so admired. Although the Legalist system prided itself on its openness to debate, debate itself was closed. Either Li Si was convinced of his own infallibility, or he had realised that his own position was just as precarious as any other's. Controversially, Li Si suggested that future generations would need to be protected from such time-wasting.

As far as he could see, the Qin empire would soon face a new problem: that of ill-informed doubt. The government ran the risk of people like Chun Yuyue believing the propaganda of previous dynasties alluding to a Golden Age that never was, and using such supposed precedents to question their rulers. Meanwhile, for as long as records endured of the former nations, there would be revolts and restoration attempts by disaffected adherents of the previous dynasties. Li Si proposed that the best way of pre-empting such problems was to remove such ideas from the heads of future scholars.

Li Si proposed a government control on knowledge itself, the removal of all books, dynastic histories and even songs that did not meet with government approval. What chance would there be of irritants like Han Fei tormenting him from the grave if there were no copies of Han Fei's works to be read? Li Si proposed the ultimate censorship, the removal of all works deemed unnecessary by the government. Mere discussion of banned works would become a capital crime, as would the hoarding of banned literature. In accordance with the strictures of Legalist justice, officials who permitted such things to go on in their jurisdiction would suffer the same punishments. Scrolls related to farming, crop management or health matters would be permitted. Songs glorifying the First Emperor would be allowed. Copies of banned literature would be maintained in the First Emperor's own library for consultation by loyal ministers, but all other editions were to be burned.[19]

It was a suggestion of terrifying moment, and an extension of government control into the very minds of its citizens. But in a sense, with the reform of the writing system, it was already under way. The First Emperor thought about Li Si's suggestion, and approved it wholeheartedly.

Li Si might have been attempting to head off potential criticism, but the First Emperor had other motives. He was losing patience with the continued excuses from his advisers on immortality, and may have hoped that a purge on wasteful and useless literature might focus the minds of his best scholars. However, even as officials seized scrolls all over the country, burning uncountable irreplaceable manuscripts, the emperor's immortality consultants continued in their charlatanry.

In 212, the immortality project was still getting nowhere. There was still no news of the marine expedition to find the Isles of the Immortals, although asides in the *Record of the Historian* imply that its leader Xufu had returned to China long ago and was lurking somewhere near Langya, frittering away the expedition's impressive budget. The First Emperor's private Taoist retreat had failed to be anything more than an expensive personal theme park. And despite the careful destruction of any documents thought to be untrue, the records of alchemical transformations still failed to bring any dragons down from the sky to transport him to heaven.

The immortality consultants were under increasing pressure. What had once been an idle boast about prolonging human life had transformed into a virtual imprisonment that kept them in perpetual fear. If they were ever found to be misleading their emperor, then their lives would be forfeit, and they found increasingly elaborate excuses to explain their poor results.

One suggested that the many expeditions in search of potions and herbal remedies were being ruined by the presence of evil spirits. His explanation implied that the First Emperor's previous wanderings in disguise had themselves been part of his magical experiments: an attempt to thwart angry ghosts by mingling with the common people. The consultant advised him that the attempted remedy had failed because, while the commoners had not known of the First Emperor's identity, there were still noble officials who had known of the plan.

The consultant suggested that the weight of the First Emperor's duties was interfering with his ability to achieve immortality. True Taoist immortals, he said, should be able to walk on water or across hot coals, but they also set aside worldly things. For as long as the First Emperor was present in the throne room or interfering in public business, he did not stand a chance of divesting himself of earthly concerns.

In a bizarre charade, the First Emperor ordered his various homes and palaces around the capital to be connected by a series of walkways and covered arcades. The result was a city-wide maze of tunnels and closed corridors, linking 277 locations. Each palace was fully furnished for the First Emperor's pleasure, with cooks, girls and guards, none of whom was permitted to leave. This situation allowed the First Emperor to choose his place of rest each night completely at random, turning up at one of the palaces without warning.

Initially it seemed like a relatively harmless, although costly, bit of fun. The First Emperor was able to disappear from public life for prolonged periods, only making himself available to Li Si and the other ministers when he wished it so. However, there were still leaks. Li Si came to meet the First Emperor on one occasion when he was at one of the outlying palaces on a hilltop. Much to the First Emperor's annoyance, he saw that Li Si's party comprised so many chariots that it could only be heading to see the ruler – in other words, Li Si had known exactly where the First Emperor would be, and was determined to arrive with enough people in his entourage to show the proper respect. On seeing the numbers of chariots, the First Emperor realised that many of his followers were only feigning ignorance of his whereabouts. He ordered the deaths of the attendants with him that day, and his wanderings remained truly secret from that point on.

Our records of the First Emperor understandably lack objectivity. They are either the glorified praises of stone monuments to his greatness, or the spiteful recollections of the dynasty that supplanted him. Consequently, it is difficult to separate folklore from fact, even in the *Record of the Historian*. But if there is a grain of truth in the Historian's claims, then the First Emperor was losing his mind. His behaviour was highly self-absorbed and irrational, his reasoning perhaps dulled by 'immortality potions', his health possibly under similar strain from the consultants' cures. His behaviour was reclusive and paranoid, both through his own fear of another assassination attempt and the consultants' pandering to it. As he reached his mid-forties, he was the most powerful man in the world, but was likely to have experienced signs of his own mortality every day.

Overindulgence and indolence were taking their toll, and the First Emperor was turning into a portly middle-aged man. For this, he was increasingly blaming the failure of his consultants to deliver on their promises. Realising that they had run out of excuses, two of the consultants made it known that the First Emperor would never find immortality while he clung to his earthly powers, and then they made a run for it.[20]

They did not get far, and their attempted escape only brought matters to a logical conclusion. Dissatisfied with years of double-talk and time-wasting, the First Emperor ordered that the full force of Qin dynasty investigation should be turned upon the immortality consultants.

It was a recipe for disaster. The interrogation methods of the Qin scribes, as recorded in the tomb of Judge Xi, were brutally scientific and logical. There was no place in the interrogation guidelines for supernatural tales or spooky threats. Each of the consultants was dragged before an interrogator and questioned about their activities. Many of the immortality treatments, in recognising the paranormal, were themselves illegal under Qin law, leading many of the consultants to enter the interview room with a crime already hanging over their heads. Many of them broke under the relentless questioning and attempted to buy leniency by implicating their fellow consultants.

Before long, the First Emperor ordered the execution of 460 scholars who had been unable to offer any evidence of their supernatural schemes. The precise method is unclear, but the text of the Historian implies that they were buried alive. Since this punishment was not on the Qin statute books, it may have been the ultimate means of testing their abilities. If any of them had magic powers, then they would surely come back to life when they were let out again.[21]

The persecution of the consultants was the last straw for one of the princes, the First Emperor's eldest son Fusu. He alone stood up to his father, arguing that the various scholars were only repeating the knowledge of ancient days, and that it was unfair to subject them to harsh persecution merely for attempting to follow his orders. Fusu's heartfelt concern was that subjects in the distant corners of the empire would grow restless upon hearing stories of such imperial excesses.

Fusu's attempt to reason with his father did not go down well. The angry First Emperor decreed that it was time for Fusu to find out for himself, and the prince was packed off in disgrace to the northern frontier, there to 'help' Meng Tian with his ongoing campaigns beyond the Great Wall.

Having exiled his son and heir, the First Emperor fell further into paranoia. In the year 211, his astronomers observed that Mars, regarded by the ancient Chinese as the 'Dazzling Deluder' had stayed within the constellation the Chinese called the Heart. This was an astrological event of great significance and could not be ignored, since such an event even had its own chapter in the *Annals of Lü Buwei*. The First Emperor was forced to deal with an omen whose terrifying qualities he would have read about as a child. The *Annals* reported the words of an adviser to an ancient duke, made the last time the astrological event had occurred: 'Dazzling Deluder is Heaven's executioner. Heart is the portion of the Heavens that corresponds to [your kingdom]. Some catastrophe awaits your lordship.'[22]

The passage from the *Annals*, designed as it was to educate, also offered a series of ways of dealing with the problem. Its allegorical subject was offered the chance to pass the curse on to his leading minister, but the lord of old refused to do so. Nor did he accept an offer to pass the curse on to his people, since if they died he would have nobody to rule. It was better, he said, for him to take the curse himself and thus preserve his land. He even refused an opportunity to pass the damage on to the harvest, as by killing the crops the curse would kill everyone else by default.

According to the folktale in the *Annals*, by admitting that his earthly lifespan was over and that he would rather die than abjure his responsibilities to his subjects, the legendary lord broke the curse. In recognition of this, Mars supposedly moved the next night through three of the lodges of the Chinese zodiac, demonstrating to the ancient astrologers that the trouble had passed, and that their lord had been granted an extension of his lifespan of twenty-one years.

However, such a happy event did not occur for the First Emperor. The *Record of the Historian* simply reports that Mars stayed in the Heart constellation. It makes no mention of any private conversation between the First Emperor and his ministers, although it is likely that they re-enacted the conversation recorded in the *Annals* in order to break the spell. But there would have been a problem: when Mars did not leap through three constellations the following night, the First Emperor would believe that the curse stayed with him and that his life was over.

There were other omens. A meteorite struck the earth in what had once been the Land of Latecoming. When imperial officials arrived to inspect it, the stone from the sky had been inscribed with a graffito that implied the First Emperor would die, and his empire would be divided back into the kingdoms of old. Although imperial investigators interrogated, and eventually executed everyone in the area, they were unable to locate the culprit.

The First Emperor attempted to combat the bad luck with a new ritual, ordering his surviving Erudites to come up with a song in praise of immortals and men who had attained enlightenment. The anthem was sung all over the empire, and was played wherever the First Emperor went, but his sense of unease did not pass.

That autumn, an imperial messenger was stopped on a road south of the Wei River, by an old man bearing a jade disc. He purportedly said that it was a gift for the 'Lord of Hao Pond' and a sign that the life of the 'Primal Dragon' was over before disappearing, leaving the disc behind.

The information was dutifully reported to the First Emperor, who recognised the disc as one he had dropped into a tributary of the Yellow River when crossing it twenty-eight years earlier, possibly on his way to his ceremony of manhood. Although the First Emperor had killed most of his supernatural advisers, he still remembered some of their stories: according to them, not even immortals could see more than a year into the future. The First Emperor now believed that he had received a message from the spirit of the River of Power itself, his watery patron deity, announcing that his life would be forfeit within twelve months.[23]

The First Emperor fell into more superstitions. Consulting the *Book of Changes*, and being advised by it to 'keep moving', he ordered for the mass movement of a number of families to new colonies and raised the ranks of every household by one level.

It had been five years since the First Emperor had last left his capital, but in the spring of 210, he announced that he would make another trip to the east. He travelled with Li Si, his trusted confidant of many years, along with the imperial entourage of servants, guards and attendants. His youngest son Prince Huhai, a boy on whom the First Emperor doted, pleaded to come along too, and the emperor agreed. With Huhai came his tutor, the long-serving eunuch Zhao

Gao, whose father had so famously saved the life of the First Emperor's father so many years ago.

The party headed far to the south before following the Yangtze downstream, disembarking from their flotilla at Danyang and heading to the sea. They had hoped to head north along the coast, but the waters of the river were so choppy and dangerous that the imperial entourage was forced to detour back towards the west over a hundred miles inland again before finding a suitable place to cross.

As the imperial party headed for its habitual summer retreat at Langya, it left behind another stone monument at Kuaizhi on the coast. If the text in the *Record of the Historian* reflects the First Emperor's original inscription, then it reads more like a last will and testament; however, the inscription may have been altered following the First Emperor's death. But the Kuaizhi monument makes a series of defensive statements, attacking the kings of old for their failures and recounting one final time the achievements of the First Emperor. It attacks unruly parents, announcing that there is nothing wrong with killing a father who acts like a rutting pig, or disowning a widowed mother who remarries; could this be a veiled reference to Zhaoji and her relationship with Lü Buwei? The final part of the inscription reads more like an epitaph, announcing that the emperor's legacy will live on.

We may gain some clue into the nature of the First Emperor's trip east from how he elected to spend his time at Langya. With curses written in the sky and falling to earth, he was going in search of one last scheme to prolong his lifespan, the long-forgotten mission of Xufu in search of the Isles of the Immortals. He found Xufu at the east coast, where the wily old man offered a series of excuses to explain why he had still not obtained the elixir of life.

Xufu claimed that yes, he had located the Isles of the Immortals, but that giant sea creatures constantly impeded his passage. Since this latest excuse tallied with a dream the First Emperor had recently had, he ordered a fishing party to set out into the sea. He went along himself, clutching a heavy crossbow at the bow of his own vessel, while other boats carried archers and spearmen. Days went past, and the imperial fishing party drifted miles west of Langya and around the headland without finding a thing.

They found something. The *Record of the Historian* simply says 'large fish', which could be anything, including sharks, whales (classified as fish by the ancient Chinese) or dolphins. Whatever they were, the First Emperor managed to kill one himself, and the fishing party returned to land to report to Xufu that the supernatural guardians had been defeated. Xufu set off towards the east in his fleet and was never seen again, although legends claim that he and his virginal crews somehow made landfall on islands far towards the rising sun and settled at the foot of a large conical volcano, Mount Fuji.

Hoping that Xufu would finally find success, the imperial party headed for home, planning to put in at Handan on the way. However, the First Emperor became gravely ill at Ping-yuan ford outside the town.

Realising that his time had come, he drafted a letter to his estranged son, Prince Fusu. He called his attendant Zhao Gao to his sickbed and dictated a simple, blunt order that would be interpreted as a tacit apology: 'Come to my funeral at Xianyang and bury me.'

The order both recalled Fusu from the borderlands to the capital and placed him as the officiator at the emperor's graveside. With that, the First Emperor lapsed into a sickness from which he did not recover. The entourage continued towards Handan, with his illness kept secret among the men, but when Zhao Gao brought food to the emperor's carriage at a place called Sandy Hill, he found him cold and dead.

SEVEN

The Ashes of Empire

The fate of the empire now rested in the hands of Zhao Gao, a man whose own father had died to save that of the emperor's father, much wronged by some of the emperor's closest friends. In his hands, he held both the emperor's final letter and the emperor's seal, and until he broke the news, nobody would know that the emperor was dead. As a loyal servant of his master, Zhao Gao was obliged to follow his last command, to send the letter to Fusu off on the long journey to the wall zone.

Zhao Gao knew what the emperor's last letter said, as he himself had been the secretary who wrote it down. The letter would cause Fusu to hand over control of the soldiers to Meng Tian and head south to Xianyang to make preparations for his father's funeral. Although brief and terse, it amounted to a pardon of Fusu's previous behaviour, an acknowledgement of the continued service of the Meng family, and, worst of all for Zhao Gao, a blessing for Fusu to take charge not only of the funeral, but of the state itself.

This was bad news for Zhao Gao. Fusu, after all, had demonstrated worrying signs of nobility and courage. He had stood up to his own father in the matter of the buried scholars, and seemed opposed to many of the principles of Legalism. If he were to return from exile backed by armies led by the Meng family Zhao Gao so despised, then there was little chance for his own cronies.

In the riskiest move of his life, Zhao Gao decided to take the news of the emperor's death and testament to Huhai – the child had been Zhao Gao's pupil, supposedly the First Emperor's favourite, and conveniently present in the late emperor's entourage. Depending on the source one believes, Huhai was either twenty-one years old or twelve; considering his tantrums and susceptibility to suggestion, it

139

seems more likely that he was a mere child.[1] In secret, Zhao Gao told him the unhappy news, and also discussed the implications of the First Emperor's letter. It appears that Zhao Gao, like many of his fellow Qin ministers, still did not agree with all of the changes that Li Si had introduced, particularly the one that forbade the king's friends and children from being set up as viceroys. Despite all the edicts and deeds of the First Emperor, Zhao Gao hoped that a Second Emperor would be more generous to his faithful servant. A kingdom or fiefdom, thought Zhao Gao, would be a good thing for him to have, and he suggested that, as one of the youngest of the emperor's many children, it might be something that Huhai would enjoy, too. But Zhao Gao warned that if Fusu took over, there would be no kingdom for Huhai. There was a chance, however brief, for Huhai himself to make a claim for the throne. The will of the emperor could be recast, after all, since others were more than used to reading it in Zhao Gao's handwriting, and the seals were still in his possession.

To his credit, Huhai is reported in the *Record of the Historian* as resisting the temptation. Following the teachings of Confucius (which must have irritated Zhao Gao immensely), he pointed out that it went against protocol for a younger son to inherit ahead of an eldest son. With something that, for once, genuinely does not seem to be the false modesty required of Chinese court protocol, Huhai refused, pointing out that he was unworthy of the position, that he doubted he had the charisma to command the Qin court, and that by accepting the subterfuge, he risked angering heaven itself.[2]

Zhao Gao, however, was used to wily diplomacy, and where Confucius was concerned there were plenty of obscure passages in the old books that offered loopholes. He pointed out that Confucius was concerned above all with what was *right*, and that there were examples in Confucius's own work of times when he approved of people who had broken those very same rules of propriety to which Huhai was now attempting to cling. Why, there were even passages in the works of Confucius where he had approved of a man who had killed his own father for the greater good. The *Record of the Historian* has Zhao Gao insisting over and over:

In great matters, one does not bother about petty formalities. With great virtue, one does not observe basic courtesies. Towns and villages each have their own customs and the hundred offices their different tasks. Thus if one pays attention to what is small but forgets what is great, he is sure to be troubled later. If one is hesitant and uncertain, he is sure to be troubled later.[3]

Zhao Gao refused to give up. In a hushed and tense few minutes, he pressed Huhai to admit that the death of the First Emperor would definitely mean danger for *someone*, and that it was his duty to himself to make sure it was not him. Eventually, Huhai agreed.

Zhao Gao next called on Li Si, and broke the news to him. Li Si, supposedly, was ready to do as the First Emperor wished, on the presumption that life under the Second Emperor would go on as before – or so claims the *Record of the Historian*, although Li Si and Fusu had famously locked horns over the Burning of the Books, and Li Si was unlikely to look favourably on his enemy's appointment as his ruler.[4] The Historian insists that Li Si was ready to support the emperor's last wish, perhaps as a symptom of Li Si's own career, which had seen a steady rise in rank and privilege from the time he arrived in Qin. Even at his most precarious moment, when he had dared to question the emperor's policy on immigrants, his words had met with imperial approval and his life had been spared. Zhao Gao, however, had endured many reversals of fortune in his life, and was all too aware of the fickle nature of an emperor's favour.

When Li Si suggested that the First Emperor's decision was rather sensible, Zhao Gao impatiently impressed upon him what might happen next, not directly but with an extended speech about the greatness of Meng Tian. Meng Tian, argued Zhao Gao, was a truly great man, one of the most competent men in the empire, a proven organiser of truly Herculean tasks, a loyal servant of the empire. But, Zhao Gao pointed out, Meng Tian was also the best friend of Prince Fusu. If Li Si expected to enjoy unprecedented access to the new ruler, he was in for a surprise. Zhao Gao urged Li Si to look ahead; with Meng Tian's qualifications and experience, he was an obvious choice for grand councillor. Li Si was now in his seventies, which would alone be enough of an excuse for him to be pensioned off, and if Li Si thought that his retirement would be trouble-free, then Zhao Gao had another surprise for him. As the First Emperor's long-serving confidant, Li Si had perhaps missed the struggle for survival among the other ministers. Life in a Legalist state might seem safe at the top, but Zhao Gao could not remember a single occasion in his twenty years of palace service in which a minister had long survived dismissal. 'Eventually,' he pointed out, 'they were all condemned to death.'

Remarkably, Li Si still took some persuading, and was ultimately reduced to tears. Li Si had become living proof of the dangers of Legalism. He had pursued harsh realities all his life and ultimately survived to see the end of his master's reign, only to be left with no idea how to fight for himself as a new generation of would-be Legalists sought to seize control. Like the First Emperor himself, he was finally gaining some inkling of his own mortality. Li Si had been successful in creating an almost perfect Legalist state, run along the lines once proposed by Lord Shang. He had used Legalism and its methods to propel Qin out of the valleys and into domination of the known world. But with the embrace of Legalism also came the survival of the fittest. In a Confucian world, Li Si might have been respected for his age and left in peace. In a Legalist world, the old and infirm were destined for the scrap heap, particularly if, like Li Si, they knew where all the bodies were buried.[5]

Eventually, Li Si agreed to join the plot, and the conspirators drafted a new letter to Fusu and Meng Tian. It was significantly longer than the dead emperor's original, and complained that in the years they had been at the border, they had failed to advance the Qin empire any further to the north – a low blow, since it had been Meng Tian's job to define the border with the wall, not push it further. Prince Fusu, moreover, had behaved in an unfilial way by repeatedly questioning his father's orders and sulking about his exile. The letter ordered that Fusu be presented with a sword with which to kill himself, while Meng Tian, for failing to report Fusu's (non-existent) plot, should similarly take his own life.

The letter made swift passage on Meng Tian's roads. When it arrived at the wall, the weeping Prince Fusu did as he was told and fell on his sword. Meng Tian, who was immediately suspicious of the sudden arrival of a messenger bearing such a grand order, refused to commit suicide and demanded confirmation that the letter had truly come from the emperor. But the letter had served its initial purpose and removed the First Emperor's chosen heir.

Meanwhile, the First Emperor's body began its progress back towards Xianyang. He had died at the height of summer, and since no embalmers could be commissioned without giving the game away, the corpse began to rot within its carriage. This was, presumably, of considerable annoyance to Zhao Gao, who was obliged to continue the charade of entering the carriage to discuss matters of state with his master. It also troubled Zhao Gao's co-conspirators, since it would only take one person to notice the smell for their plot to be discovered. Accordingly, they arranged for a fish cart to be placed sufficiently close to the First Emperor's carriage to mask the stench with something just as unpleasant, but not so suspicious.

News of Prince Fusu's suicide reached the cortège as it neared home, leaving Zhao Gao and Li Si free to carry out the rest of their plan. On their arrival at the capital, they solemnly announced the First Emperor's demise and his unexpected deathbed nomination of Huhai as his successor.

With Huhai crowned as the Second Emperor, the body of his father was laid to rest in a mausoleum beneath Mount Li, surrounded by statuary and memorials to his greatness. The tomb had been under construction for some time, although some of the Second Emperor's early acts ordered for work on several annexes, since he ensured that tombs were required for many of his siblings. The Second Emperor also journeyed to Mount Tai to offer his own respects to the gods. Now installed as palace prefect, Zhao Gao was determined to settle old scores, and advised his former pupil to make the notoriously tough Qin laws even tougher. Although there were already some provisions for punishing entire families for one person's misdeeds, Zhao Gao advised extending the criteria.

Just as the First Emperor's advisers once strove to erase the past, Zhao Gao advised similar purges. Meng Tian's brother Meng Yi, who might have stopped the whole sorry usurpation bid had he not been ordered away from the First Emperor's side to pray for his recovery, was one of the first victims. Zhao Gao's other targets were people in similar positions to undermine his stolen authority. Perhaps rightly, considering the deception, he regarded the Second Emperor's greatest threats as issuing from within his own family, and concocted a number of excuses to do away with his brothers. Twelve of the First Emperor's other sons were framed for unspecified crimes and executed, their bodies displayed in the marketplace like common criminals. Nor did the Second Emperor spare his sisters, allowing Zhao Gao to have ten of them killed and their property confiscated. It is possible that the sisters were not the main target, but rather their husbands, since many of the First Emperor's supporters had been granted princesses as brides. Thanks to the increased harshness of the laws, Zhao Gao was able to remove many of his own rivals by directing false accusations against their wives. By the end, Zhao Gao did not even bother to put much effort into the trumped-up charges. Like Prince Fusu before them, three of the Second Emperor's siblings found themselves arrested without warning and held in the inner palace at Xianyang. A messenger eventually arrived to tell them that their behaviour had been criminal and that they were ordered to die. They were clearly surprised at this, since the *Record of the Historian* includes their protestations: they had never argued with Zhao Gao, they had maintained all the temple appearances and sacrifices required of them, and they had always carried out their orders without question; what, precisely, was their crime? The messenger reportedly shrugged that orders were orders and that the reason was not included; the tearful boys went to their deaths.[6]

Zhao Gao's purges reached such terrible levels that one of the First Emperor's last surviving sons decided to turn himself in before he could be framed. Suspecting that he would be next on the hit list, the high prince was initially tempted to flee, but knew that such an act would spell death for his family. Instead, he submitted a memorial to the Second Emperor announcing his wish to follow his father into the afterlife, as a filial son should.

The *Record of the Historian* reports the Second Emperor and Zhao Gao cackling with glee at the thought of an enemy prepared to remove himself before they had even attempted to deal with him. The Second Emperor willingly granted the prince's request to die and added to the graves surrounding the tomb of the First Emperor, construction of which had begun long before the death of its resident, and was still continuing into the reign of his successor. However, the Second Emperor was soon diverting manpower from his father's mausoleum and sending the work-gangs on other tasks. Work continued on the road network, including the appropriately named Straight Road, which reached up to the northern borders of Qin, and the Speedway, a long conduit to the far south and east, with a central lane walled off by parallel tree lines, and supposedly reserved for the emperor's sole use. Such schemes were merely a continuation of the First Emperor's policies, although another venture was less immediately useful. This was the Apang Hall, a truly massive building that could seat 10,000 people, with a four-sided pyramidal roof 11 metres above the crowd. The foundations of its walls and outer gardens are still extant, and describe an area of 144 square kilometres.[7] The Apang Hall was a reflection of the heavens; it was to represent the Pole Star, while its various outlying colonnades seemed to have been designed in an attempt to map out the constellations overhead. It was a bold, sweeping gesture, turning part of the Qin capital itself into one giant star map, since one colonnade reached all the way back across the Wei River into Xianyang itself. The work required timber from Sichuan and south of the Yellow River, and stone from distant mountain quarries, and the hall itself, had it ever been completed, would have been impressive indeed.[8]

The *Record of the Historian* implies that the Second Emperor overstretched his resources and the goodwill of his people. Although no mention was made of it during the Second Emperor's lifetime, it was not lost on later dynasties that the first syllable of his birth-name, Huhai, was that same *Hu* that had been predicted as a destroyer of the empire. Perhaps, whispered the superstitious, the prophecy had referred not to the barbarians of the frontier, but to the ruinous behaviour of the Second Emperor.

But while Zhao Gao's settling of scores led to many deaths at the court, and the severity of the Qin system continued, it is difficult to comprehend how the public works of the Second Emperor were any more or less arduous than those of the First – indeed, Huhai was only working to his father's grand plan; the reason given for his attention to the Apang Hall is his unwillingness to leave one of his father's projects incomplete.[9] Possibly it was a matter of distance; a Great Wall sounded grand, and the hardships of its construction were conveniently far removed from society, less exciting when the slaves and the work-gangs were labouring in the next street. If the Second Emperor's plans turned the capital into a building site, it was not welcomed by the townsfolk, many of whom had been forcibly relocated there by his father. However, it is more likely that the unrest of the Second Emperor's reign was merely a delayed backlash to that of the First.

The first revolt broke out in 209 in what had once been the Land of the Immaculate. Its alleged catalyst, much to the embarrassment of any surviving Legalists, was the law itself. Chen She, a former farm worker who had been conscripted into the army and worked his way up through the ranks, had been placed in joint charge of leading one of the innumerable Qin slave-gangs to a new posting, only to discover that they would be arriving late. Chen and his fellow officer, so the story goes, realised that they now faced an unpleasant choice between the death penalty for the dereliction of duty or desertion.

The story might be true, although it would require a considerable increase in the severity of Qin laws in the two years since the First Emperor's death. Even considering the clampdowns instigated by Zhao Gao, it seems unlikely that a sergeant would face execution simply for turning up late. Extant Qin laws from the grave of Judge Xi tell us that Chen She and his colleagues would have probably faced a fine rather than death, although Chen She's later actions might have predisposed him to exaggerate the excesses of the Qin dynasty.[10]

Before long, Chen She was claiming that he was not merely dodging a criminal sentence, but leading a righteous revolt against the Second Emperor in the name of the wronged Prince Fusu. Fusu was long dead by this point, but news could travel at a sluggish pace among the commoners, particularly if it had been carefully suppressed. Chen She's uprising soon changed in character, losing any pretence of supporting a Qin candidate, and instead aiming at the overthrow of the Qin dynasty itself. Chen She announced that he was the new king of the Land of the Immaculate, a call to patriotism that helped fuel the fire of rebellion elsewhere. In fact, he was already doomed. The new 'king' lasted barely six months before he was murdered by one of his own men in an argument over his change in attitude towards his fellow rebels. However, the private arguments of Chen She and his lieutenants made little difference to the public face of the revolution – other parts of the Land of the Immaculate rose up in support, and news drifted in to the Qin capital that similar revolts had sprung up in the Land of Swallows, the Land of the Devout and the Land of Latecoming.[11]

The immediate problem was nearer to hand: an army of rebels approaching the Qin capital, led by one of Chen She's associates. Somehow, the rebel army had managed to get close without running into any Qin defenders, although the terse passages of the *Record of the Historian* hide an even more unpalatable prospect, that Qin's supposed defenders had probably swelled its ranks. Without the means to summon more distant troops in time, the Second Emperor turned to desperate measures. He authorised Zhang Han, the construction manager at his father's tomb, to free thousands of the workers from their chains. Criminals were promised pardons and slaves their freedom if only they would fight.

Weapons were in short supply, since the government had already gathered up surplus swords and axes to make the great statues of the Qin capital. Instead, Zhang Han ransacked part of the First Emperor's own monument, grabbing swords from the hands of the army of terracotta statues that stood symbolic guard. Construction on the tomb was abandoned, and Zhang Han's ramshackle army somehow beat back the attackers. It bought the court much-needed time to call in other forces, and soon reinforcements were added to Zhang Han's army as he pursued the rebels into the Land of Late-coming. With the first rebel leaders dead, Zhang Han pressed his campaign on another pretender, and then another, drawing the struggle further and further from the Qin heartland.[12]

The experience frightened the Second Emperor, who readily took Zhao Gao's advice to stop showing himself at court. While the Second Emperor cowered in his private chambers, Zhao Gao began to exert even more authority, claiming to speak for his master, even on policy decisions that went against common sense.

Realising that Zhao Gao's incompetence and the Second Emperor's indecisiveness were threatening everything he had worked for, Li Si made repeated attempts to arrange a meeting. His chief complaint was with Zhao Gao, and Zhao Gao controlled access. Zhao Gao cunningly ensured that Li Si dug himself ever deeper into trouble. Instead of refusing point blank to allow him to meet the emperor, he instead arranged so that Li Si was kept waiting for long periods, only to have his request for an audience delivered whenever the emperor was about to start eating. The emperor only grew irritated with what he saw as Li Si's lack of consideration, and openly refused to see him. Eventually, Li Si submitted a written memorial, signed by at least one other high official, urging that the Second Emperor make stronger efforts to deal with the rebellion, instead of wasting time and manpower constructing a monument. It would seem that the Apang Hall was a particular issue with the court; the Second Emperor was determined to complete it in his father's honour, despite reports of revolts in the eastern provinces.

The Second Emperor's official reply had all the hallmarks of its probable author, Zhao Gao. Deliberately taunting Li Si by quoting from his late rival Han Fei, it pontificated about days of old and the need to honour one's ancestor. Instead of answering Li Si's complaints, it made vague pronouncements about the glory of the First Emperor and the need to show respect to him and his successor.

Meanwhile, Li Si was under attack from other quarters. The rebellions had originated in what had once been his home state, the Land of the Immaculate; in fact, the first revolt had begun in the county next to Li Si's birthplace. Li Si's own son was the prefect of the Three Rivers commandery, over which an entire rebel army had somehow managed to pass unchallenged. Whispers at court suggested that Li Si and his family were somehow implicated in the rebellion.

Zhao Gao reminded the emperor that Li Si had been one of the conspirators over the matter of the First Emperor's will, but that while everyone else involved had managed to gain rank and influence, Li Si was stuck where he was, at the highest possible level of government. There was simply no way to reward Li Si beyond making him a king in his own right, and, Zhao Gao sneakily suggested, perhaps this had occurred to Li Si himself.[13]

It was the final straw. The Second Emperor authorised the interrogation of Li Si to investigate the matter more thoroughly, and Zhao Gao gleefully ordered the grand councillor's arrest. Li Si was interrogated using the same approved methods set down in the legal books recovered from Judge Xi's grave, that is, allowed to explain himself and then pressed upon those facts that did not seem to add up. However, since Zhao Gao was the interrogator, and he had already decided what the answer would be, the Qin law then authorised torture. Now an old man in his seventies, Li Si received a thousand lashes before he eventually agreed to whatever it was that Zhao Gao wanted him to say.

Zhao Gao used the false confession to secure Li Si's dismissal, and his own promotion to grand councillor. Li Si was sentenced to endure the Five Punishments, a cocktail of tortures that would find him tattooed, mutilated, maimed, castrated and eventually beheaded. Awaiting punishment in his prison cell, Li Si wrote one final memorial to the Second Emperor, sarcastically phrased as a series of further confessions to non-existent crimes. If it was a crime, wrote Li Si, to turn the state of Qin into the ruler of the world through hard-fought battles and hard-won diplomacies, then he was undoubtedly guilty. If it was somehow wrong to strengthen the state with detailed programme that unified language, weights and measures, then Li Si had been caught red-handed. If it was a crime to honour his ruler with worship and sacrifice, to oversee public works and to ensure that the people loved their ruler, then no man was more guilty than Li Si.[14]

It was a persuasive, pointed argument, easily the equal of Li Si's famous memorial on the importance of immigrants. If it reached the ear of the Second Emperor, it might sway him as its predecessor had swayed his father. But Zhao Gao took one look at Li Si's scroll and set it aside – prisoners, he said, were not allowed to write to their ruler.

Li Si's sentence was carried out in a slightly altered form; it was ordered that he, his wife and children should be hacked in half at the waist, in full public view in the marketplace of the Qin capital. His last recorded words were spoken to his weeping son, likely himself to have been in his fifties, as the pair went to meet their executioner. Li Si looked back on his life before Qin, when he had lived in the Land of the Immaculate and gone out with his son, then a young boy, and their old yellow dog to hunt rabbits near their house. Perhaps regretting time spent on politics instead of family, he wryly noted to his son that even if they wanted to go hunting today, they would not have the chance.

Just as Li Si was brought down by Zhao Gao's intrigues, other servants of the dynasty sensed the time was right to save themselves. Those who could have saved the Qin dynasty were now either dead, like the Meng family of generals, or defecting. Rebel forces in the Land of Latecoming captured Wang Li, the grandson of the great general Wang Jian, quite possibly to his own great relief. Zhang Han, the general who had somehow turned a bunch of slaves into a fearsome army, met with several close calls and sent repeated dispatches back to the capital asking for reinforcements. When none were forthcoming, he turned himself over to one of the new pretenders. His army switched sides with him. Even as Zhao Gao continued to kill off everyone who stood in his way, and workers continued to toil on the pointless majesty of the Apang Hall, reports drifted in of ever greater numbers of rebel victories. Before long, one of the many rebel armies was sure to march through the passes into the Qin heartland, and it seemed unlikely that anyone would be able to stop them. By this point, all the former vassal states were now in revolt and at least six pretenders now claimed to be king in their respective states.

Now standing unopposed, Zhao Gao continued his efforts to keep the Second Emperor out of sight. The *Record of the Historian* recounts a strange incident that may have been a symbol of Zhao Gao's supreme authority, or perhaps a cruel means of confusing an already addled mind. He supposedly presented the Second Emperor with a deer, telling him that it was a horse.

The Second Emperor laughed and corrected Zhao Gao, only to find all the other attendants were in on the deception; they all assured him that he was looking at a horse.

Now convinced that he was suffering from delusions, the emperor was persuaded to confine himself to his quarters, fasting and occupying himself with hunting trips and other distractions. He was, understandably, also troubled by nightmares, telling Zhao Gao that he dreamed his carriage had been attacked by a white tiger, which killed one of the horses. Zhao Gao interpreted it for him with more mystical diversions, telling him that he was under the curse of Evil Water, which needed to be fought off with further prayers and sacrifices. Zhao Gao advised a country trip, in the course of which the emperor should throw four white horses into a nearby river and thereby break the spell.

Bundled out of town on the pointless mission, the Second Emperor became so jittery that when he saw a human figure in the trees on his hunting grounds, he immediately shot him.

Zhao Gao made an earnest show of covering up the accident, arranging with the prefect of the capital (conveniently, his own son-in-law) to announce the discovery of a corpse with no clue as to the assailant. However, in private, he berated the emperor for his manslaughter of an innocent bystander and warned him that unless he left the palace, the gods would punish him.[15]

By this point, however, the Second Emperor was growing angry. Frustrated with the stories of revolts in the outside world, he lost his temper and chastised Zhao Gao. It was a relatively small deed, simply the arrival of a messenger informing Zhao Gao that the emperor was unhappy with developments. However, it was a fatal error for the Second Emperor, who had thus far been tolerated as a convenient figurehead for Zhao Gao. By flexing his imperial muscles, he had just demonstrated that he was too dangerous to continue in his role.

The conquered nations had reverted to their independent state. The Qin empire was over, within a few years of the First Emperor's final victory. Zhao Gao, however, was prepared to make the best of a bad situation. If Qin was no longer an empire, it could be a kingdom again. He could arrange it so that the Second Emperor took the blame, and perhaps explain that imperial ambitions were an offence against heaven and had been punished. All he needed to do was remove the Second Emperor and replace him with a more pliable ruler – a new *king* of Qin, not an emperor.

A mere three days after the Second Emperor had relocated to his country retreat, Zhao Gao arranged for members of the palace guard to dress as bandits and feign an attack on the residence.

The last battle of the Qin empire was a brawl at a country house, with the Second Emperor's eunuchs and attendants on one side and the disguised soldiers of the palace guard on the other. Several dozen died in the scuffle, until the Second Emperor was left cowering behind the curtains in his chambers.

Even the *Record of the Historian* cannot decide on exactly what happened next. It presents two versions of the same event. In one, Zhao Gao permits the emperor to flee to a high tower, and then persuades him to jump rather than face capture by what he claimed were 'bandits'.

In the other version, the Second Emperor found himself alone with a single remaining eunuch. He asked his last faithful servant why he had not warned him before, and the eunuch replied that the emperor had killed everyone who had tried to warn him, and that staying silent had been the only way of staying alive.

Zhao Gao's son-in-law entered the chamber, flanked by archers and guardsmen. They read out the accusations levelled against the Second Emperor: that he had failed in his imperial duty, performed badly as a ruler, and lost the Mandate of Heaven. The Second Emperor pleaded to see Zhao Gao, but his request was refused.

Instead, the prefect ordered that the Second Emperor 'take appropriate steps'.

Perhaps seeing Zhao Gao's plan to downgrade Qin to a humble kingdom once more, the Second Emperor offered to resign his imperial status. When this was refused, he instead suggested that he be pensioned off with a noble title. When even this was refused, he begged to be allowed to live as a commoner, as he had supposedly permitted some of his relatives to do so.

The prefect realised that he had perhaps not made himself clear. He told the Second Emperor that the sentence was death. As the guards approached to carry it out, the Second Emperor killed himself.[16]

What happened next is also a subject of debate. One ancient account claims that Zhao Gao took the emperor's seal and announced that now he was the ruler of Qin. Much to his annoyance, however, the assembled nobles refused to obey him, and he was forced, with great reluctance, to put a member of the royal family back on the throne.[17]

In a council of the surviving nobles and ministers, Zhao Gao announced that the empire was gone. Instead, he nominated a young prince, Ziying, as the new king of Qin, hoping thereby to cancel any difficulties on the other side of the passes. If the ruler of Qin no longer claimed to rule the world, then presumably Qin would be spared the need to fight off any rebels.

Prince Ziying's exact identity is unclear. One account calls him a younger brother of the First Emperor, another calls him a nephew of the Second. His credentials, however, were impeccable, as was his grasp of court politics. King Ziying knew all too well that Zhao Gao had only enthroned him with the greatest reluctance, and he had already seen what happened to those who got in Zhao Gao's way. There were already whispers at court that Zhao Gao had received messengers from the Land of the Immaculate, offering to recognise him as king of Qin. Unless Ziying acted quickly, Zhao Gao could all too easily trump up some new charges, or, worse, arrange for an invasion from the Land of the Immaculate to instal himself on his 'rightful' throne. Accordingly, Ziying immediately confined himself in his quarters, feigning sickness and thereby avoiding a trip to the local temple that might have been an attempt by Zhao Gao to arrange an assassination.

When Zhao Gao eventually came to pay his respects to Ziying, the king stabbed him to death and ordered his relatives to be executed. By then it was too late, armies were already marching on Qin. A mere forty-six days after his enthronement, the last king of Qin was forced to ride out to surrender before one Liu Bang, who had, like Zhang Han, once been a gang-master on the construction of the First Emperor's tomb. Liu Bang led a force of 3,000 into the Qin capital, killing any remaining defenders and carrying off the children as slaves. Liu Bang's troops had red uniforms, the former colour of Qin criminals, itself a reference to the ruling element of the former Zhou dynasty – Fire.

Fire is what Liu Bang brought to the Qin capital, razing it to the ground in a conflagration that engulfed the entire city, including the legendary Apang Hall and the irreplaceable library of banned books. With that, Qin was truly gone. Ziying and his family were soon executed and China was plunged back into civil war.

Although the domain of the First Emperor was no more, his ambition continued to inspire others. It was only a few years after the destruction of the Qin capital that Liu Bang would return, to build again on the opposite bank of the Wei River. This new town would become Chang'an, the capital of a new emperor and a new dynasty. The dynasty was the Han, and its first emperor would be Liu Bang.

In less than a decade, the 10,000-year plan of the First Emperor had been destroyed.

EPILOGUE

The Terracotta Army

On a spring day in 1974, the workers' collective of Xiyang village decided that the weather was good enough to continue the regular well-sinking operation. A work party set out to find a good spot – the region around Mount Li was riddled with underground springs and watercourses, and every little extra helped when it came to irrigating the fields. There was a song in the local area that appeared to acknowledge *something* below the ground:

> Iron picks chop, one and again
> Dig, dig down to the crystal hall
> Striking fear into the dragon king
> Make him bow
> Make him scrape
> Promise water, thirst to slake.

But the locals knew there was no such thing as dragons or palaces below the ground. Demand for water was growing with the swelling population, so that once-small well-digging projects were now quite large. Yang Peiyan, the diminutive leader, and his lofty relative Yang Wenxue, led their diggers west from the village, through an orchard of persimmon trees to the base of a steep rise. The locals called the area 'the southern waste' because neither they nor their ancestors could remember any time when they had been able to get any crops to grow there. Persimmons were the best they could manage, but just because the soil was poor, it didn't follow that there wouldn't be water there.

The two Yangs sketched a circle in the ground with their pickaxes, ready for the morning when the dig would begin in earnest. Seven members of the Yang family were back the next day, to strip away the thistles and creepers on the ground, and began digging, confident that they would eventually break through into the underground watercourse known to head towards a nearby valley.

Two days later, the Yangs hit earth that seemed supernaturally hard. Although they did not know it at the time, they had reached a wall of rammed earth made by one of the Qin dynasty work-gangs 2,000 years before that had lost none of its hardness. The Yangs, however, persisted, chopping through the super-tough earth until they reached another layer, tinged red and black. This, later archaeological surveys have concluded, was the ash and dust from the great fire that destroyed much of the First Emperor's mausoleum in the unrest after the death of the Second Emperor. At the time, the brothers thought it could be an old forgotten kiln (which would explain the fired soil), or perhaps even an old foundation from a forgotten building. As digging continued and the Yangs argued over what they were doing, on 23 March 1974 Yang Zhifa suddenly found something: a circle of clay that he initially mistook for the neck of a pot. In fact, it was the neck of a terracotta soldier, long separated from its head.

In the Yangs' story of their discovery, there are hints of earlier finds long forgotten or suppressed, since it was apparently a local tradition that ancient pots were very useful. Instead of hacking through the soil as they had been doing for days, the Yangs slowed down, hoping to extract this old 'pot' from the earth intact and use it for storing eggs or some other foodstuff.

When they could establish that the item they had found was not a pot at all, but a terracotta figure, they assumed that it was a leftover from a local Muslim rebellion. It was only when they finally reached the brick floor of what turned out to be an underground chamber that they realised they had found something even more interesting.

The Yangs' well-digging exercise transformed into an archaeological dig, much to the annoyance of the local Party representative, who arrived towards the end of March demanding to know why they had not yet found water. On being shown the bricks, he ordered an immediate halt, realising but not quite comprehending that the bricks of the chamber floor were Qin dynasty, even though they seemed to be far too distant from Mount Li to form any part of the First Emperor's tomb.

Similar disbelief greeted the local governor. For centuries it had been assumed that the First Emperor's mausoleum centred on Mount Li itself, and yet the finds of the well-diggers were far from it. The well now forgotten, the soil from the initial dig was sifted, unearthing more terracotta pieces, and the fragments of what might once have been crossbow trigger mechanisms.

By that June, the news was out. Something had been found near the site of the First Emperor's mausoleum, and if a find of the magnitude of the Yangs' was present so far from it, the size of the necropolis itself may have been grossly underestimated.

There was clearly something beneath the ground at the Mount Li site, enough to have led to a special protection order in 1961 signed by Chairman Mao. However, the order only covered the obvious part of the mausoleum, the area enclosed by its wall, and did not recognise the land beyond it as part of the site. We now know that the necropolis stretched for many acres beyond the boundaries believed to have existed in 1961.

The First Emperor's 'ten thousand generations' barely lasted a few years past his death, but his successors improved upon his ambition. Liu Bang's Han dynasty lasted, give or take a couple of succession squabbles, for four hundred years. Liu Bang himself ordered in 195 BC that 'twenty households' should move to the site of the Qin emperor's mausoleum to watch over the tomb. To this day, twenty villages sit in the immediate vicinity of the mausoleum, one of them the hamlet where the Yang family lived; the terracotta army may have been rediscovered by the distant descendants of the people left to guard it.

In the intervening centuries, not even the Han dynasty lasted. It was followed by other civil wars and other unifications. Sometimes, new border regions asserted control – tribesmen from beyond the wall proclaimed themselves emperor on several occasions, including the Mongols in the Middle Ages, and the last conquerors, the Manchus. China reached its greatest extent during the Manchus'

Qing dynasty, lasting from 1644 until the twentieth century. The last emperor was finally deposed, replaced first by a republican government and then the communists who rule mainland China to this day.

These later dynasties improved upon the wall building of the First Emperor, only adding to his mystique, but while the Qin dynasty was regarded as the first of China's historical rulers, it was not regarded as the greatest. There was simply no evidence of what it had achieved; historians were left with nothing but the legends and stories of ancient chroniclers and occasional pieces of archaeological evidence.

Every dynasty, however, had its stories of the First Emperor. Ban Gu, the historian of the Han dynasty, corroborated the stories of the First Emperor's tomb, and reported that its outer façade had been destroyed in a fire by one of the armies that overran Qin. He also implied that it was not long before looters descended upon the rubble, and that after they had departed, the site was abandoned. What outer evidence of the tomb still remained was burned in a second blaze, this time started by a shepherd searching for a sheep in one of the access tunnels, and rashly doing so with a torch that set fire to the façade.[1]

Six hundred years after the death of the First Emperor, the geographer Li Daoyuan told another story. He explained that Mount Li had been chosen as a site for its auspicious geology: it had once had a gold mine on its north face and a jade mine on its south face, demonstrating not only its sacred value, but also perhaps how the tunnels had come to be dug in the first place. Li Daoyuan also mentioned that the tomb had been thoroughly gutted, claiming that 300,000 men (a number suspiciously similar to the work-gangs said to be stationed there) had spent a month stripping it bare, and still left items behind. He also repeated the shepherd story, claiming that the ruins had smouldered for three months before the fires finally died out.

During the Ming dynasty, over a thousand years after the death of the First Emperor, the site was still a place of legend. A government official reported that the inner and outer walls of the tomb complex were still in evidence, although the gates in them were long gone. Grave markers and entrances to underground silos could be found all over the site, but local legend held that the tomb of the First Emperor himself was not in the complex, but within the hill of Mount Li behind it.

There are, however, some strange contradictions in the stories about the destruction of the tomb. The most notable is the description of the initial robbing, seemingly conducted as an ongoing military operation by one of the generals who would later fight to become an emperor himself. Ancient records make much of the burning of the Qin capital, but have nothing to say about the emperor's coffin. If it had actually been found, surely it would have been reported? When ancient writers speak of the looting of the complex, they are discussing an area several miles across, which would have been scattered with pavilions and temples, each probably adorned with works of art, fine furnishings and precious items. And yet, in all this discussion of the pillaging, there is no mention of any traps (which the emperor's grave was supposed to contain), nor any discussion of the First Emperor's actual sarcophagus. Is it possible that, despite the claims of ancient scholars, the looters had merely pilfered the façade yet failed to find the tomb itself?

Later poets and singers mention a gold coffin laying undiscovered, but still acknowledged that the site had been well and truly plundered by 2,000 years of passers-by. The location of the coffin may have been a secret, but not so the terracotta army, which must have been accessible enough for Zhang Han's men to pry the swords from the hands of the statues before they went to defend Qin in its last days. Even if the central part of the necropolis lay undisturbed, surely the terracotta army must have warranted a mention over the intervening millennia?

Apparently not. From the state of the finds at the Mount Li site, we now know that the terracotta army was incomplete. Zhang Han's army may have even comprised the very potters and artisans who were supposed to be finishing it, instead deserting it with an entire grave pit left empty. In the modern museum at Mount Li, the figures have been painstakingly pieced together, but the army did not stand to attention when it was first discovered. Instead, it was lying in pieces, smashed by the men who had built it as they scavenged it for weapons, then probably crushed by the falling roof beams of a later fire.

Although the scale of the terracotta army was not known until the 1970s, there were several foreshadowings of its discovery. Up to 5 metres of reddish, sandy soil had accumulated over the site in the centuries since its construction, but archaeologists also found evidence of earlier, impromptu discoveries. During the digs at Mount Li, archaeologists found several graves from the eighteenth and nineteenth centuries, whose diggers had obviously struck terracotta fragments, only to discard them as worthless with the rest of the back-filled soil.

The region around Mount Li had been left untouched for a long time, but was repopulated during the sudden expansion of the Chinese population during the seventeenth and eighteenth centuries. It may be a mere coincidence that there are now twenty villages around the complex, or perhaps new settlers used the wells of earlier communities, and naturally gravitated to the places where the original guardians once lived. But the growth in population of modern times led to new inhabitants, new settlements and new disturbances of the earth. It was only after the terracotta army had been discovered that the relevance of earlier finds made sense – numerous peasant tales of 'bits of pot' turned up by ploughs or found in wells. One local legend, which only made sense with hindsight, was that well-diggers on Mount Li itself had fallen into a vast cave stacked with human skeletons and other bones. However, when a second party was sent to investigate, the cave could no longer be found. Terracotta remained the material of choice for many devotional objects and religious statues, a fact which would naturally lead anyone finding fragments that they were imminently about to stumble upon a grave or cursed site. Such superstitions probably preserved many of the terracotta sites, including some that have yet to be found.

One old farmer from a homestead near the Mount Li site confessed a childhood memory of his father, who spent days digging a well, only to uncover a terracotta figure. In a mixture of twentieth-century cynicism and traditional superstition, the man angrily dragged the terracotta figure out of the ground – according to his son, Huo Wanchun, the figure was apparently complete. The terracotta figure was then hung on a nearby tree and attacked with sticks by local boys, in an attempt to 'exorcise' the magical curse that had somehow prevented Huo's father from finding water.

The countryside around Mount Li is riddled with similar finds, not only of the famous terracotta figures, but also of the fragments of the necropolis – roofing tiles, bricks and chunks of masonry. A local song remembered a bygone age when a fashion developed among well-to-do locals to collect Qin dynasty bricks, ensuring that evidence of the actual buildings was soon eroded further, as the materials of their construction were carted off to build forgotten follies and garden ornaments elsewhere. Local superstition held that using a Qin brick as a pillow would prevent fevers and toothaches, a belief that led to brisk business for local scavengers, but the further displacements of archaeological evidence.[2]

In twentieth-century China, there were even more premonitions of the find. In 1932, a few paces from the western wall of the mausoleum, a farmer found a terracotta head only a couple of feet below ground level. The government of the time, however, pre-occupied with its own corruptions and threats, had no interest in the find, which was eventually lost. The site suffered further abuse in the 1940s, when republicans converted it into a makeshift fortress during the civil war with the Chinese communists, rending its base, sides and summit with protective trenches. In 1948, shortly before Chairman Mao proclaimed the foundation of the People's Republic of China, peasants in the nearby village of Jiaojia found two terracotta figures, thought to have been crouching crossbowmen or half-kneeling stable-boys. Although the mood of the time was iconoclastic, the figures fell into the hands of village elders, who maintained some degree of traditional superstition and placed the figures on the altars of a nearby temple. They eventually came to the attention of government officials around 1956, and were cited in a report of the time as the only extant examples of the statuary of the

First Emperor's legendary mausoleum. At the time, writer Zheng Zhenduo rightly guessed that they formed part of some kind of symbolic honour guard for the First Emperor, and that there were others somewhere else to be found.[3]

The terracotta army, and its impressive scale, was unearthed at an important moment in China's history. Chairman Mao, who had led the Chinese nation in several ill-advised Great Leaps, was dying, taking stock of his life and searching for historical parallels. The mysterious First Emperor, who had united China in spite of itself, who had forced unification of currency, language and measurement, who had caused untold suffering in the hope that he could beat all the swords into ploughshares (or statues), was hit upon by Chairman Mao as a fitting historical analogy for him to draw with himself. Even as parties of archaeologists continued to excavate around the Mount Li site, cronies of the Chairman were revisiting old stories and legends of the First Emperor, suggesting that his ultimate achievement had been to unite the workers of China for a greater good – a fitting epitaph for a communist leader, even though the people of Red China were expected to identify less with the emperor than with the disaffected workers who deposed his successors.

It is expected that the excavations of the Mount Li site will take years, if not decades. Already, a generation has passed since the initial discovery, and still archaeologists have barely scratched the surface. So far, over 7,000 terracotta soldiers have been discovered, many decked out in the studded armour of the First Emperor's palace guard. Standing at the front were archers and crossbowmen, flanked by more archers, charioteers and infantrymen, with heavily armoured soldiers bringing up the rear. Many of the soldiers are empty-handed, lending credence to the story of Zhang Han's pilfering of the site in order to mount a defence against rebels. A few still have swords in their hands – still sharp after 2,000 years, fashioned out of a rare alloy of thirteen metals.

In 1976, archaeologists uncovered two further pits to the north of the first discovery. The L-shaped Pit 2 contained a mixed squadron of warriors, including crossbowmen, infantrymen and soldiers in

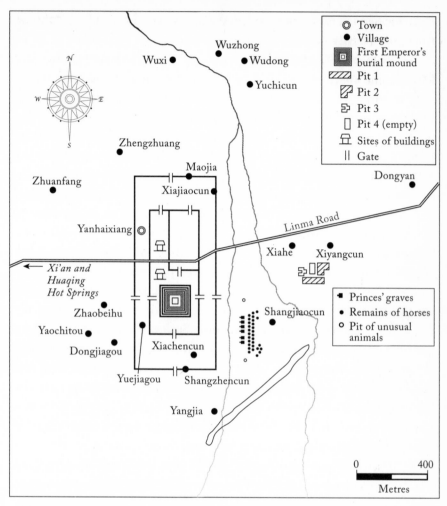

The site of the First Emperor's tomb. (After Zhang, *The Qin Terracotta Army*)

robes. At its southern end were eight columns of war chariots, complete with terracotta horses, although the wooden chariots have long since rotted, and could only be re-created by guessing what may have sat in between their remaining bronze artefacts. From the layout of the formations, it seems that each chariot functioned as a transport, base and possible supply dump for a group of soldiers. They were not weapons in their own right, but served by attendant spearmen for defence, and may have also carried arrows or quarrels to supply nearby archers.

To the west end of Pit 2 is a cavalry unit, comprising not only further chariots, but also 108 saddled horses, led by their bridles by men presumed to be their riders. The cavalrymen were armed with crossbows, implying that they were used more as mobile, mounted archers than as knights – the stirrup was invented long after the time of the First Emperor, and its absence made mounted charges less effective. All of the soldiers in Pit 2 seem to be arranged differently from their counterparts. Some are standing to attention as if on parade, while others (the archers) appear to be practising. Whatever their disposition, they, like the soldiers of Pit 1, all faced towards the east, the place of the First Emperor's conquests and the origin of the forces that would overthrow his successors.[4]

The U-shaped Pit 3 was much smaller than the other two, but contained a command unit. A charioteer stood at the reins of his horse-team along with three officers. Beside the chariot team, an ante-room led to a stable area, confirming archaeologists' suspicions that many more pits and symbolic buildings awaited discovery under the modern ground level, dotted all around the mausoleum site. Beside the stables were ante-rooms guarded by still more terracotta soldiers, armed with strange weapons like adzes, wooden shafts with a heavy, cylindrical bronze lump, its business end chopped into a rudimentary point like that of a modern drill bit. Such weapons were vicious, heavy-duty maces for use in close combat, with ends designed to punch through the armour of anyone who dared to come so close. Perhaps they were even designed to stun instead of kill, since anyone who made it this far might be a spy or assassin, and could be kept alive for interrogation. Beyond the guards lay the remains of what had once been a curtain rail, presumably holding up a thick tapestry to separate the command room from eavesdroppers. In the general's inner sanctum, evidence was found of sacrificed animal bones; it was intended not merely for strategy meetings, but for victory prayers and sacrifices.[5]

Most notably, however, the command unit's leading officer did not seem to be present, although Pit 3 sits close to an as yet unopened tomb that may contain, or have been intended for, a general – perhaps even one of the associates of the First Emperor who were framed so soon after his death, Meng Yi or even Meng Tian.

The most lavish armour was reserved for the officer corps, their ranks further denoted by bright coloured scarves and patterns of two, three or four tassels on the front and rear of their body armour. Leading officers did not have weapons in their hands; instead they rode in their chariots with their large war-drums, carrying batons to beat out signal codes to the men. From the evidence found in the Qin tombs, the act of drumming the signals was done by the generals themselves, so presumably they, too, were the men who obtained the infamous 'blood for the drums'.[6]

Most of the officer class in the Qin army have beards or moustaches, although facial hair is thought to have been a sign of their greater age rather than of a particular fashion worn for the sake of rank. Their hats, however, changed depending on their rank, with pheasant-feather headdresses for the leaders. Many of the soldiers have hair braided in elaborate patterns, suggesting that they wore it habitually long, knotting it into thick mats before battle both to keep it out of the way and to afford a little extra protection. Archers' hair was usually knotted to the left in order to give them a better line of sight if shooting right-handed – it also, presumably, was less likely to block the line of sight of another right-handed archer standing behind. Remarkably, it is even possible to determine a racial origin in many of the warriors – their facial features have much in common with the present-day inhabitants of the region, particularly Sichuan, Shaanxi and other north-western prefectures.[7]

Although the terracotta army has, so far, been the most impressive single event, and elements of the main tomb remain a mystery, we should remember that archaeology prizes not just the treasures, but the people who built them. The area of the Qin tomb was home to many thousands of artisans, labourers and slaves over a long period, and hence is still revealing elements of their daily life. The remains of a fishpond were discovered early on, as well as minor finds, such as temple bells and dropped coins.

On the eastern flank of the necropolis, outside its walls, archaeologists uncovered a north–south row of six smaller graves, possibly containing the remains of the princes brought down by Zhao Gao. Ahead of the graves are the remains of twenty-nine horses, possibly a random number, or perhaps the same horses that drew funeral carts for the luckless princes.[8] Pits of rare animals, including peacocks, sit to the north and south of the small graves, and other objects have been found all over the site.

Remarkably, the findings of the late twentieth and early twenty-first century have confirmed many of the claims made in the *Record of the Historian*, not about the army itself, which is not mentioned in detail, but about the disposition of the site. Underground barriers protect the ground beneath the site from springs, as mentioned in the Historian's account. The site was incomplete, with a 'Pit 4' sitting empty next to the other, more famous discoveries. The terracotta army was buried in underground halls, a symbolic re-creation of the First Emperor's own attendants, and would have remained untouched were it not for a fire that brought roof beams crashing down upon chambers below.

However, the First Emperor's tomb still remains a mystery. A cynic might suggest that, considering the vast size of the site, it is a cunning marketing ploy to leave the tomb unopened, particularly since so much circumstantial evidence suggests that it may have already been robbed in the distant past. The museum may have much of interest to the tourist, but archaeology itself is a slow process, its benefits not immediately apparent, and in constant danger of reductions in funding. For as long as the First Emperor's tomb sits in the distance behind the exhibition hall, the guides have stories to tell their parties, and the managers have promises to dangle before funding bodies. If the archaeologists were to fall immediately upon the tomb mound, the magic of the First Emperor could be over before it has really begun – the archaeologists would find plenty to occupy them, but if the tomb were a wreck and the treasures plundered, there would be no twenty-first-century Tutankhamen mystique left to sell.

The terracotta army was a private secret, a series of underground chambers designed for the First Emperor's use in the afterlife, but ransacked before completion and left smashed into millions of pieces. It now stands reborn, with a purpose-built chamber overhead that lets in daylight the army was never supposed to see, not even in the original plans. Its nearby exhibition hall features imitation pagoda roofs built of steel and faced in granite, using materials much more solid and longer lasting than the wood and clay structures of old.

Visitors are told that the First Emperor himself has yet to be found, although the place of his repose is visible to all. Somewhere, they say, beneath the green-leafed mound in the distance, the First Emperor is said to lie at the centre of a vast model of the universe, with a ceiling into which jewels have been set as constellations and, 'under heaven', a sculpted replica of the mountains and plains of the known world, from the wastes beyond his Great Wall to the jungles and mountains of the barbarian south, rivers picked out in mercury running down to a replica of the ocean. Someday, the guides claim, our shovels will finally reach the chamber, and we will see the giant candles of whale oil that were designed to burn for a century. We will find the piled corpses of the tomb's builders and, beyond them, the luckless concubines, sacrificed because no man but the First Emperor could be suffered to love them.[9]

The greatest prospect of all is that the guides are right. So much of the fanciful reporting of the *Record of the Historian* has been proved true since 1974; why would the Historian Sima Qian lie about everything else? The lootings reported in days gone by, the scavenging, the fires and chamber collapses, do not necessarily refer to the tomb itself, but all seem to apply to the vast symbolic army to be found at the foot of the hill. The terracotta army may have inadvertently performed its chief function, guarding its lord by distracting his would-be grave robbers. Although no contemporary images of the First Emperor survive, we may yet get to see his face, as he lies in his undiscovered burial chamber, in a golden coffin set on a silvery sea.

GENEALOGICAL TABLES

1. Ancestors of the First Emperor

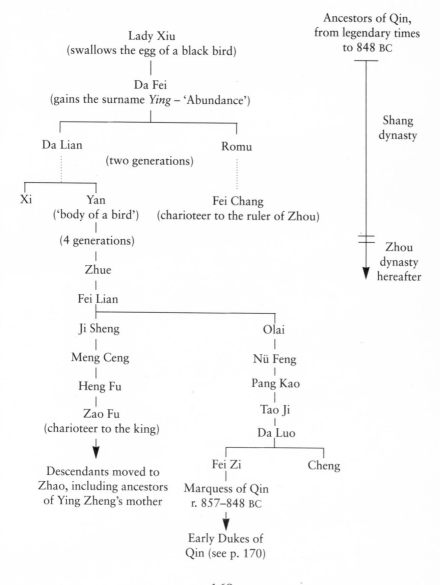

Lady Xiu
(swallows the egg of a black bird)

Da Fei
(gains the surname *Ying* – 'Abundance')

Da Lian   Romu

(two generations)

Xi   Yan   Fei Chang
('body of a bird')   (charioteer to the ruler of Zhou)

(4 generations)

Zhue

Fei Lian

Ji Sheng   Olai

Meng Ceng   Nü Feng

Heng Fu   Pang Kao

Zao Fu   Tao Ji
(charioteer to the king)   Da Luo

Descendants moved to   Fei Zi   Cheng
Zhao, including ancestors
of Ying Zheng's mother   Marquess of Qin
                              r. 857–848 BC

                              Early Dukes of
                              Qin (see p. 170)

Ancestors of Qin,
from legendary times
to 848 BC

Shang
dynasty

Zhou
dynasty
hereafter

2. *Early Dukes of Qin, 857–621* BC

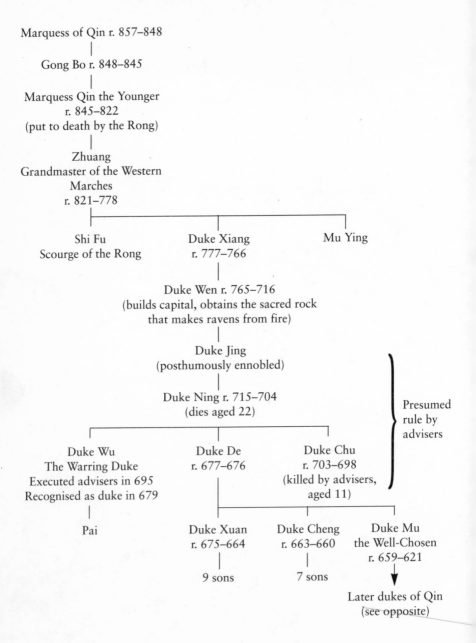

Marquess of Qin r. 857–848
|
Gong Bo r. 848–845
|
Marquess Qin the Younger
r. 845–822
(put to death by the Rong)
|
Zhuang
Grandmaster of the Western
Marches
r. 821–778

Shi Fu · Duke Xiang · Mu Ying
Scourge of the Rong · r. 777–766

Duke Wen r. 765–716
(builds capital, obtains the sacred rock
that makes ravens from fire)
|
Duke Jing
(posthumously ennobled)
|
Duke Ning r. 715–704
(dies aged 22)

Duke Wu · Duke De · Duke Chu
The Warring Duke · r. 677–676 · r. 703–698
Executed advisers in 695 · (killed by advisers,
Recognised as duke in 679 · aged 11)
|
Pai

Duke Xuan · Duke Cheng · Duke Mu
r. 675–664 · r. 663–660 · the Well-Chosen
| · | · r. 659–621
9 sons · 7 sons

} Presumed rule by advisers

Later dukes of Qin
(see opposite)

3. *Later Dukes of Qin, 621–338* BC

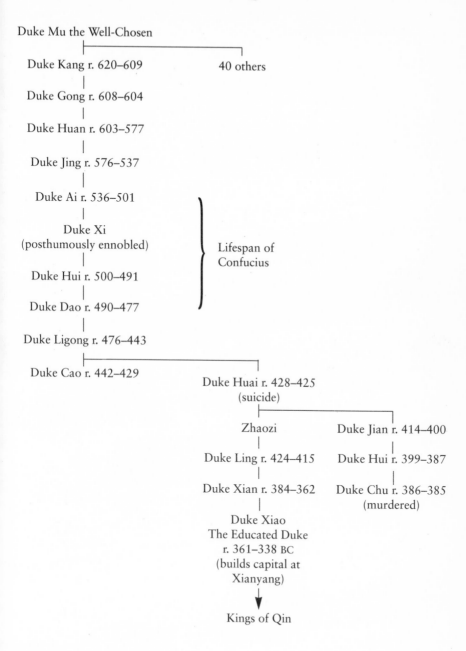

Duke Mu the Well-Chosen

Duke Kang r. 620–609   40 others

Duke Gong r. 608–604

Duke Huan r. 603–577

Duke Jing r. 576–537

Duke Ai r. 536–501

Duke Xi
(posthumously ennobled)

Duke Hui r. 500–491   Lifespan of
                                       Confucius

Duke Dao r. 490–477

Duke Ligong r. 476–443

Duke Cao r. 442–429

Duke Huai r. 428–425
(suicide)

Zhaozi   Duke Jian r. 414–400

Duke Ling r. 424–415   Duke Hui r. 399–387

Duke Xian r. 384–362   Duke Chu r. 386–385
                              (murdered)

Duke Xiao
The Educated Duke
r. 361–338 BC
(builds capital at
Xianyang)

Kings of Qin

4. *Ying Zheng's Immediate Family*

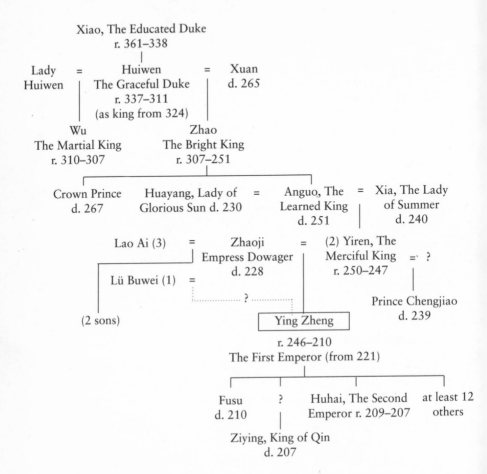

Xiao, The Educated Duke
r. 361–338

Lady Huiwen = Huiwen The Graceful Duke r. 337–311 (as king from 324) = Xuan d. 265

Wu The Martial King r. 310–307

Zhao The Bright King r. 307–251

Crown Prince d. 267

Huayang, Lady of Glorious Sun d. 230 = Anguo, The Learned King d. 251 = Xia, The Lady of Summer d. 240

Lao Ai (3) = Zhaoji Empress Dowager d. 228 = (2) Yiren, The Merciful King r. 250–247 = ?

Lü Buwei (1) =

?

Prince Chengjiao d. 239

(2 sons)

Ying Zheng
r. 246–210
The First Emperor (from 221)

Fusu d. 210

?

Ziying, King of Qin d. 207

Huhai, The Second Emperor r. 209–207

at least 12 others

5. *The Meng Family, Companions of the King*

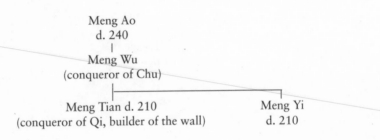

Meng Ao
d. 240

Meng Wu
(conqueror of Chu)

Meng Tian d. 210
(conqueror of Qi, builder of the wall)

Meng Yi
d. 210

172

APPENDIX I

Names and Titles

Packaging Chinese history into a legible account is rendered extremely difficult by the Chinese language itself. A Chinese character is not a meaningless 'letter', denoting a single sound. Instead, it is a complex glyph packed with meaning, an entire syllable with a tonal dimension completely lacking in English. To an oriental reader, a single word like Qin, Rong or Di means much more on the page than it ever can in its simple romanised form. This presents unexpected complications for the popular historian, flensing meaning from sentences and leaving us with monosyllabic moments like: '*Dan*, prince of *Yan*, feared the king of *Qin*.' More irritatingly, without the ability to convey tonal structure or the inherent meaning of the characters, there are barely 120 *words* in Chinese. The number of men called *Li*, or countries called *Wei*, soon build up in any account, further confusing the reader. There is a world of difference between *wéi* and *wèi*, but it is often not obvious to the non-Sinologist.

The Chinese of the period had several kinds of names. The *ming* is the name given at birth, and the *zi* is an 'adult name' conferred upon reaching maturity (for boys) and on marriage (for girls). People also had a *xing*, or surname, denoting their family, and some, particularly nobles, had a fourth name, or *shi*, denoting their clan affiliation. Nobles also received a posthumous name, conferred in summary of their life's achievement. When faced with such a plethora of titles, I have endeavoured to assign a single name to each major character and to stick with it to preserve editorial consistency and reader sanity. In *First Emperor*, I have followed the policy of my earlier Chinese history books, *Pirate King* (published as *Coxinga* in paperback) and *Confucius*, diligently removing any Chinese words

173

where possible. I have, in translation terms, mixed communicative and referential language, rendering what things *mean* rather than what they *say*, on those occasions where it makes the text more readable. I have also deliberately applied anachronisms where they help simplify the text, preferring the term *Sichuan*, for example, to the archaic provinces of Shu and Ba, even though *Sichuan* only entered popular parlance in the thirteenth century AD.

Such a policy works, I hope, in a popular account, but requires an appendix such as this so that readers may pursue the same story in other books. This requires not only giving the entire, unsullied names of the historical participants, but also their renderings in another romanisation system – I have used the Pinyin system invented in the twentieth century, but many earlier accounts use Wade-Giles, the nineteenth-century system cluttered with apostrophes and strange consonantal transformations, that spells Beijing as 'Peking', yet still expects the reader to pronounce it as 'Beijing'. There is still another system, Yale, which is an even better representation of the sound of Chinese on the page, but seems so alien to non-specialist eyes that it might as well be Martian. This is probably not a good time to mention that in the 2,200 years between the time of the First Emperor and our own, many of the pronunciations of Chinese characters have shifted so much that they are almost unrecognisable. The meaning of a character may still be apparent to modern Chinese eyes, but the sound it might have once made can be the subject of much conjecture and debate.

In the text, I have been judiciously careful with my use of the terms *king* and *emperor*. Strictly speaking, the subject of this book was indeed the first emperor of China, creating a new title by combining two characters used to describe the rulers of old – *huang* and *di*. Some sources describe the legendary holders of those titles as 'emperors' rather than the more semantically correct 'kings'. Furthermore, it might be argued that the ruler of the failing Zhou dynasty, in claiming to be the ruler of all under heaven, might also be termed as an emperor, even though he wielded temporal power more equivalent to a pope or United Nations Secretary General. But the 'ruler' of the Zhou is better described as a king, as are the rulers of the separate states who, in the generations preceding the events of this book, gradually began repudiating his authority by taking the title of king for themselves. It was the Qin emperor who conquered and united these warring states, creating both the concept of a ruler above these minor satraps who required a new title, and indeed ultimately the name for the region he himself controlled – China.

Anguo (An-kuo). His name means 'Peace (or Safety) for the King-dom', and his posthumous title as ruler, Xiaowen, is translated here as the Learned King.

Chunshen (Ch'un-shen), also known as Huang Xie (Huang Hsieh).

Educated Duke, Xiao (Hsiao).

Fan Yuchi (Fan Yü-ch'i).

Gao Jianli (Kao Chien-li).

High Prince. Ying Gao (Ying Kao), called simply 'High' in my text to avoid confusion with Zhao Gao.

Jieshi (Chieh-shih) – literally 'stone tablet'.

Jing Ke (Ching K'o).

Lady of Glorious Sun, Huayang, Queen Dowager Huayang.

Lady of Summer, Xia (Hsia), Queen Dowager Xia.

Lao Ai, also *Lao Du*. The name suggests an individual of 'licentious and poisonous behaviour', which is hardly an auspicious title. One suspects that Lao Ai, if he existed at all, must have been a nickname for the true individual whose name has been erased from history by disapproving scribes. Shortly before his fall from grace, Lao Ai was created Marquess Zhangxin (Chang-hsin), ironically 'the long-trusted'.

Li Si (Li Ssu).

Lü Buwei. I often refer to him by his given name, Buwei, rather than his monosyalbic surname Lü.

Mu the Well-Chosen. 'Well-Chosen' is my translation of *Renhao* (Jen-hao), literally 'A Good Appointment'.

Red Prince. He is called *Dan* (Tan) in original sources, which is also the name for cinnabar; occasionally the Crown Prince of Yan (Yen), or Prince Tan of Yen.

Wuyang. More properly Qin Wuyang (Ch'in Wu-yang). I have

referred to him chiefly as plain *Wuyang* in order to avoid confusing his surname with the name of the nation of Qin in the text.

Xu Furen (Hsü Fu-jen). A *furen* is a 'master' of an art, so this could be either a proper name or a mark of respect for his smithing skills. The name is recorded in the *Record of the Historian* as that of the man who sold the world's sharpest dagger to the Red Prince.

Yiren. Sima Qian calls him Zichu, but according to the *Intrigues*, he was originally called Yiren (Yi-jen), 'the Outsider', and renamed Child of Chu, *Zichu* (Tzu-Ch'u) by the Lady of Glorious Sun in honour of his diplomatic decision to wear the national dress of Chu, her native country, when he went to seek her support. Upon his enthronement, he was known as King *Zhuang Xiang* (Chuang Hsiang), a coinage combining the characters for Sobriety and Assistance that I have translated as 'Merciful' in the light of certain acts conducted during his reign and recorded by Sima Qian.

Zhaoji. She is strangely unnamed in ancient sources, or at least is identified by terms so descriptive as possibly not to be names at all. Some call her *Zhaoji*, which simply means the Lady of Zhao. Another source calls her *Geji*, which could mean Princess of Songs, but is also a poetic term for a performer – roughly equivalent to *chanteuse*. Considering her former career, it is possible that the *Record of the Historian* refers to her disparagingly as the Singer. She is also referred to as the 'Queen Mother' until Ying Zheng's grab for imperial power, whereupon she becomes the 'Empress Dowager'.

APPENDIX II

The First Emperor on Screen

The First Emperor remained a taboo subject for much of the twentieth century in China, although he enjoyed a brief renaissance in the early 1970s, as supporters of the ailing Chairman Mao lent credence to his image as a despot with his country's best interests at heart. However, since the uncovering of the terracotta army and its attendant archaeological evidence, we now know more about the First Emperor and his times than the inhabitants of any generation since his own. It is not the place of a historical account to turn to evidence from modern media, but it is perhaps worth noting that for the grandest and most accurate evocation of the First Emperor's life and times available in the twenty-first century, the reader may find a trip to the cinema as useful as a trip to a museum.

The Qin Emperor TV series (1984) is the longest version available, stretching over sixty episodes and starring Lau Wing as the emperor. It is also the least realistic, clinging to the *Record of the Historian*'s claim that Lü Buwei was the father of Ying Zheng, which leads Zhaoji to carry the First Emperor in her womb for eleven months. The series introduces the convenient character of Mi, a girl from Han over whom Ying Zheng and the Red Prince quarrel. Mi leaves Ying Zheng at the altar to elope with the Red Prince, although she dies during their escape, thereby instilling into the Red Prince a desire for revenge. When her younger brother eventually arrives in Qin to plead for his country's future, he is revealed as the stuttering Han Fei. Meanwhile, the Red Prince's younger sister turns out to be a secret agent and martial artist, who falls in love with Jing Ke and herself dies trying to avenge him after the assassination attempt fails. As if that were not enough dramatic licence, the final chapters find Ying Zheng falling in love with the wandering widow

Meng Jiang-nü, and touring his empire hand-in-hand with her until she develops a guilty conscience over her dead husband.

The film *The Emperor's Shadow* (Qin Song, 1996) focuses on the story of the musician Gao Jianli, taking the reference in the *Record of the Historian* to his early life in Handan and combining it with elements of the story of the Red Prince. In fact, the film suggests that Gao Jianli's mother was a wet-nurse, making him and Ying Zheng 'milk-brothers'. When the assassin Jing Ke arrives for his audience with the king, he is almost sent away, but claims to have a personal message from Gao Jianli in order to get close enough to make his attempt on the king's life. Gao Jianli is captured in the fall of Yan and (literally) branded as a criminal in a misunderstanding, but attracts the attentions of the First Emperor's disabled daughter Yueyang; as with all other modern dramatisations of the events in the *Record of the Historian*, the crucial extra ingredient is always romance. The emperor commissions Gao Jianli to compose a national anthem suitable for the Qin state, and rashly allows him to believe that he can marry Yueyang when she has already been promised to the general Wang Ben.

The Emperor and the Assassin (Jing Ke ci Qin Wang, 1999) concentrates on the plot of the Red Prince and introduces the character of the First Emperor's favourite concubine, his childhood companion who wishes that they could return to their carefree days in Handan, and who agrees to help in his intrigues in the hope that he will have more time for her if he unites the world. The Red Prince is *allowed* to escape and goaded into mounting an assassination plot, because that is the only way that the First Emperor will have an excuse to invade the Land of Swallows. Meanwhile, the Lao Ai conspiracy is presented in a reversal of historical events as a small band of revolutionaries overwhelmed by vastly superior numbers of loyalist troops. *The Emperor and the Assassin* also inserts many scenes about the life and motivation of Jing Ke, presented as a reluctant killer who has sworn off all fighting after witnessing a blind girl's suicide. The First Emperor himself plans the elements of his assassination as if it is a form of theatre, and goes into the throne room on the day wearing armour under his robes. Jing Ke's attack proceeds as described in the *Record of the Historian*, but the First Emperor is left angry that none of his followers dares to intervene. He is also deserted by his concubine, who has come to believe in the assassin's aims.

Barely two years after *The Emperor and the Assassin*, the actor who played Jing Ke (Zhang Fengyi) would portray Ying Zheng himself in the TV series *First Emperor* (Qin Shi Huang, 2001), which would also use the idea of a concubine from the emperor's native Zhao as a catalyst. Running for eight months and over thirty episodes, the series stretches mere sentences from the *Record of the Historian* into entire episodes, and speculates wildly on the machinations concerning the selection of Ying Zheng's principal wife. As with its predecessors, it homes in on the most glaring absence in the Historian's biography, the First Emperor's love life, since he somehow managed to sire twenty children without more than a passing reference to his wife or concubines. The TV series suggests a conflict between the Lady of Glorious Sun, who favours a candidate from her native Chu as her adoptive grandson's bride, versus Zhaoji and Lü Buwei, who push the First Emperor into choosing a princess from their native Zhao. The emperor's decision is swayed by the presence of his childhood sweetheart, Li Jiang, as a handmaiden in the entourage of the Zhao princess, although he later develops an interest in Ah-ruo, the Chu princess he previously spurned. The series grapples with the absence of the emperor's women from the historical record by pointing out, logically, that only a princess was worthy of an emperor in marriage, but that in dethroning all the rival dynasties, the emperor had left himself unable to allow for any woman to be of suitable rank. 'The only princesses left,' he admits at one point, 'are my daughters.' *First Emperor* also dwells at length on the rebellion and defeat of Ying Zheng's younger brother Chengjiao, an incident swiftly glossed over in the *Record of the Historian*, but reasonably presented here as an early attempt by Zhaoji and Buwei to put a more pliable puppet on the throne. Its later episodes are presented as a family drama: the Zhao princess commits suicide to avoid capture by her enemies, leaving Li Jiang as the emperor's favourite concubine and the stepmother of Prince

Fusu, although she refuses to become empress because she cannot bear the hatred of Ying Zheng's enemies. Ah-ruo, meanwhile, achieves a greater role as a symbol of all Ying Zheng's failings. As the mother of the hated Huhai, she is the instrument of Qin's decline, and haughtily tells her husband that, like the Chu nation itself, he may have conquered her body, but her heart remains her own. The series departs further from historical events with a final confrontation between Li Si and Prince Fusu on the Great Wall. Li Si confesses his deception over the First Emperor's will, but then uses his legendary powers of persuasion to convince Fusu to commit suicide as ordered to preserve the future of Qin; if Fusu takes the throne, he argues with inadvertent irony, the empire will not last.

The movie *Hero* (Ying Xiong, 2002) presents a considerably more symbolic and fictionalised account of the assassination plots against the First Emperor, within a framing device distantly inspired by Jing Ke's throne-room deception. A sheriff arrives at the palace, claiming to have dispatched three assassins, although the trophies he bears of his achievement are merely a ruse to get within striking distance of the First Emperor himself. However, in a marked move from previous accounts, the would-be assassin has a change of heart and recognises that despite the terror and death tolls inflicted by the emperor, China is better off with him than without him.

Notes

Prologue

1. Confucius, *Analects*, XV, 11.
2. Watson, *Records of the Grand Historian*, pp. 58–61; Nienhauser, *Grand Scribe's Records*, VII: 325–32. Both books are partial translations of the *Shi Ji*, which I translate in my own text as *Record of the Historian*. Hereafter, Nienhauser references are given as *GSR*, and my own translations from the *Shi Ji* as *SJ*.
3. Watson, *Records of the Grand Historian*, p. 60. The time is not specified, but was long enough for a Qin general to annex an entire nearby kingdom, and for the news of the neighbour's defeat to reach Yan. At the very least, Jing Ke's lordly delights took several weeks. An anonymous, fictionalised account from the first century BC, perhaps using a source now lost to us, places Jing Ke's sojourn with the Red Prince at three years. See 'Prince Tan of Yen', in Bauer and Franke, *Golden Casket*, p. 44. A variant account can be found in Crump, *Chan-kuo Ts'e*, pp. 504–11.
4. Bauer and Franke, *Golden Casket*, p. 44. Disc-shaped coins were only used in the Land of Swallows *after* the Qin conquest. At the time of the Red Prince's plot, Yan coins were knife-shaped and unlikely to be much good for skimming.
5. Watson, *Records of the Grand Historian*, p. 61.
6. *Ibid.*, p. 62. I have changed Watson's *Ch'in* to *Qin* to avoid further confusion.
7. The evidence for this is wholly circumstantial – the fact that the fight over the chess game is recorded at all, and the later passage in which Lu Goujian, on hearing of the assassination

attempt, says: 'What a pity that he never properly mastered the art of swordsmanship. And as for me – how blind I was to his real worth!' Reading between the lines, Lu Goujian may have received an invitation from Jing Ke, but ignored it, unaware of its true meaning until it was too late. Watson, *Records of the Grand Historian*, p. 66.

8. Watson, *Records of the Grand Historian*, p. 62. Crump, *Chan-kuo Ts'e*, p. 509, distinguishes two songs, not one that is repeated. Yoshikawa, *Shin no Shikôtei*, pp. 97–8, has a much longer song, supposedly by Jing Ke, but dating from the eastern Jin dynasty long after the events took place.

9. *SJ*, p. 324.

10. Wirgin, *Emperor's Warriors*, pp. 85–6.

11. Some sources interpolate a passage in which Jing Ke seizes the king and demands that he swear to abide by his demands on pain of death, in the style of a famous would-be assassin of antiquity. The tale of 'Prince Tan of Yen' goes even further, claiming not only that Jing Ke's blade wounds the king, but also describing an uneasy stand-off in the courtroom. The king asks to hear a final song, and a minstrel delivers a coded message in her lyrics that allows him to fight off his assailant. The story omits to explain how the king might have survived the supposedly deadly poison, or indeed what concessions Jing Ke might hope to obtain, and sounds suspiciously like the set-up to a musical number in a forgotten play. Whatever its origins, it does not appear in the *Record of the Historian*, which alone is probably reason enough to discount it. See *GSR*, VII: 331; Bauer and Franke, *Golden Casket*, pp. 47–8.

12. The *Record of the Historian* reports cryptic last words from Jing Ke, that he only failed in his attempt on the king's life because he had made the mistake of offering a deal. There is, however, no evidence of this deal beyond the discounted earlier passage mentioned above. *GSR*, VII: 332; Crump, *Chan-kuo Ts'e*, p. 510.

Chapter One

1. Yuan, *Dragons and Dynasties*, pp. 1–13. The evocative translation of Ban Gu (P'an Ku) as 'Coiled Antiquity' is from Birrell, *Chinese Mythology*, pp. 30–1, although she cannot trace any use of the name before the third century AD.
2. Yuan, *Dragons and Dynasties*, p. 19.
3. *Ibid.*, p. 45.
4. *Ibid.*, pp. 55–6.
5. *GSR*, I: 90n.
6. *GSR*, I: 91.
7. See however *Analects*, IX, 13 (Clements, *Confucius*, p. 98), where Confucius muses that even a barbarian state might benefit from his guidance.
8. *GSR*, I: 107.
9. Knoblock, *Xunzi*, I: 17–18.
10. *GSR*, VII: 95; Crump, *Chan-kuo Ts'e*, p. 81.
11. Knoblock, *Xunzi*, I: 18. (Qiangguo, 16.4.)
12. *GSR*, VII: 89.
13. *GSR*, VII: 95.
14. Cotterell, *First Emperor of China*, pp. 107–8.
15. *GSR*, I: 111.
16. Sage, *Ancient Sichuan and the Unification of China*, pp. 116–17.
17. Bodde, 'The State and Empire of Ch'in', p. 47. See also *GSR*, I: 114, which suggests that the king's injury was a broken shinbone, leading to later fatal consequences.
18. Knoblock and Riegel, *Annals of Lü Buwei*, p. 17.
19. Yao, *Introduction to Confucianism*, p. 76.
20. Cotterell, *First Emperor of China*, p. 96.
21. Knoblock, *Xunzi*, III: 223.
22. Knoblock, *Xunzi*, I: 17.
23. Crump, *Chan-kuo Ts'e*, p. 129.
24. Knoblock, *Xunzi*, I: 20.
25. He may have written anonymous memorials during this period that were later incorporated into the *Annals of Lü Buwei*.
26. Crump, *Chan-kuo Ts'e*, p. 151.

27. *SJ*, p. 306.
28. *Ibid.*, p. 306. 'A hundred years on' is a euphemism for the death of her husband.
29. Crump, *Chan-kuo Ts'e*, pp. 151–3.
30. *SJ*, p. 308, uses *qi*, the usual term for weeping, preceded by *fei*, a character that usually means 'boiling'.
31. Sima Qian, *GSR*, I: 123, suggests it was instead in honour of his ancestor Zaofu, whose descendants adopted the name of his fief, Zhaocheng, as a surname. It is, however, curious why he does not use Ying – since that would be a more obvious choice. The surname Zhao seems to imply that the mother's family was of higher birth than the father's and certainly contributed to the rumours concerning his parentage. It should also be noted that a suspiciously similar story was told about Lord Chunshen of Chu, Land of the Immaculate, who supposedly tried to pass off his own son as the king's. Perhaps the tales became confused during the unrest that led to the beginning of the Han dynasty.
32. *SJ*, p. 308.
33. Yoshikawa, *Shin no Shikôtei*, p. 31. The quote is from the 'Wu xing zhi' (Five Elements) of the *Han Shu*, a book designed to pick up Sima Qian's history where it left off. Typically, however, the *Han Shu* keeps to arch insinuations; if we believe such nonsense (and stranger things have happened in the Qin dynasty!), it is equally probable that Ying Zheng's name was deliberately changed to Zhao Zheng temporarily in an effort to break the supposed curse.
34. Yuan and Xiao, *Tales of Emperor Qin Shihuang*, p. 11. The servant was Zhao Sheng; his son, Zhao Gao, would go on to become the Second Emperor's tutor and, ultimately, murderer.
35. *GSR*, I: 83.

Chapter Two

1. Knoblock and Riegel, *Annals of Lü Buwei*, p. 12. Crump, *Chan-kuo Ts'e*, pp. 66–7, translates them as the Nine Cauldrons, and reveals that they were massive bronze ceremonial objects once used by the rulers of the ancient Shang

dynasty, and subsequently appropriated by the ancestors of the Zhou. The tripods/cauldrons were widely regarded as signifiers of divine kingship, and were also the subject of a theft attempt by the state of Qin's chief rival, the state of Qi.

2. Hung, 'Preparations for Unification', p. 51.
3. *Lüshi Chunqiu*, 17.2; Knoblock and Riegel, *Annals of Lü Buwei*, p. 417.
4. Knoblock and Riegel, *Annals of Lü Buwei*, p. 46.
5. *GSR*, VII: 335.
6. Bodde, *China's First Unifier*, p. 14.
7. *GSR*, VII: 313n.
8. Hung, 'Establishment of a New System', p. 107.
9. Knoblock and Riegel, *Annals of Lü Buwei*, p. 12.
10. Di Cosmo, *Ancient China and Its Enemies*, p. 142.
11. *SJ*, p. 311.
12. Knoblock and Riegel, *Annals of Lü Buwei*, p. 21. The possibility still remains that Sima Qian may have written the passage, perhaps before his castration when such information would not have been known to him, or that events happened exactly as described, with the hair-plucking merely used as a means of fooling those in immediate contact with Lao Ai in the early days of his deception.
13. Kronk, *Cometography*, p. 7.
14. *GSR*, I: 129.
15. *GSR*, I: 93, 130. Yoshikawa, *Shin no Shikôtei*, p. 50, convincingly argues that the journey to Yong, the old Qin capital, is mentioned by the Historian because Ying Zheng's manhood ceremony would have taken place there. Since this was also the location of Zhaoji's new residence, it is possible that the ceremony led to a number of family secrets coming out: Lü Buwei's attempts to hang on to the regency, Ying Zheng's desire to take it, and Lao Ai's affair with Zhaoji.
16. Crump, *Chan-kuo Ts'e*, p. 420. Wade-Giles converted to Pinyin.
17. *GSR*, VII: 315, quoting the *Shuo Yuan*.
18. *GSR*, I: 130. On *guixin*, 'gathering firewood', see Hulsewé, *Remnants of Ch'in Law*, p. 15. For the length of the sentence, see *GSR*, I: 132, which has Ying Zheng exempting the Sichuan

exiles from '[further] state service' in 235, tellingly after the final purges that followed the funeral of Lü Buwei.

19. Knoblock and Riegel, *Annals of Lü Buwei*, p. 25, quoting the *Shuo Yuan*. Cottrell's *Tiger of Ch'in*, p. 128, suggests that Ying Zheng issued such a command with a naked sword lying ominously across his lap, and a man-sized cauldron bubbling away in the corner of the throne room ready to boil any transgressors.
20. Bodde, *China's First Unifier*, p. 18.
21. *Ibid.*, p. 19. I have converted Bodde's proper nouns from Wade-Giles, as his original text was written before the Pinyin romanisation system had been invented.
22. *Ibid.*, p. 20.
23. *GSR*, VII: 315.

Chapter Three

1. Knoblock and Riegel, *Annals of Lü Buwei*, p. 26.
2. *GSR*, VII: 223.
3. *GSR*, VII: 230. The murder of Lord Chunshen also caused Xunzi, the former teacher of both Li Si and Han Fei, to lose an administrative post in Chu. See *GSR*, VII: 184.
4. Bodde, *China's First Unifier*, p. 72.
5. Kronk, *Cometography*, p. 7. The *Record of the Historian* mentions no more celestial phenomena until 213, the year of the Burning of the Books, which we may reasonably assume to be a record from the later Han dynasty and not something recorded by the Qin administration. See also, Cotterell, *First Emperor of China*, p. 156.
6. Crump, *Chan-kuo Ts'e*, p. 448, reports an admission of the state of Han's buffer value by Queen Dowager Xuan, the First Emperor's great-grandmother, in a fourth-century incident where Qin sent troops into Han to support the local aristocracy in the resistance of an invasion from Chu. As a native of Chu, Xuan was unlikely to have been very happy about it.
7. Landers, 'Political Thought of Han Fei', p. 16.
8. Bodde, *China's First Unifier*, p. 40. (HFZ 49.)

9. Lo, 'Restoration and Counter-Restoration', p. 65.
10. *GSR*, VII: 26–7.
11. Bodde, *China's First Unifier*, p. 63
12. *Ibid.*, p. 65.
13. *Ibid.*, p. 68. Ch'in converted to Qin for consistency.
14. Crump, *Chan-kuo Ts'e*, p. 158. Wade-Giles 'Chao' converted to Pinyin 'Zhao'.
15. *Ibid.*, p. 159.
16. *GSR*, VII: 29.
17. Loewe, *Biographical Dictionary*, p. 201.
18. Crump, *Chan-kuo Ts'e*, p. 503.
19. *Ibid.*, p. 155.
20. Bauer and Franke, *Golden Casket*, p. 31.
21. *Ibid.*, p. 38.
22. Hung, 'Success of Unification', p. 79.
23. Crump, *Chan-kuo Ts'e*, p. 349.
24. *Ji*, the 'Place of Thistles', would eventually be rebuilt, and is better known today as Beijing.
25. *GSR*, I: 133.
26. *SJ*, p. 330.
27. Yuan and Xiao, *Tales of Emperor Qin Shihuang*, p. 77. Yuan and Xiao faithfully repeat the error of the original *Record of the Historian*, which places Meng Tian at the head of the relief forces, even though he was still a government scribe at this point. I have, however, corrected the name to Meng Tian's father Meng Wu, following Loewe, *Biographical Dictionary*, p. 437, and *GSR*, VII: 363.
28. *SJ*, pp. 330, 332.
29. *SJ*, p. 332. Some translators might prefer 'pacified', but Ying Zheng uses the term *dading*, which has no element of 'peace', but rather an enforcement of his rule.

Chapter Four

1. *SJ*, p. 334.
2. Hung, 'Consolidation of Unification', pp. 109–11.
3. Knoblock and Riegel, *Annals of Lü Buwei*, p. 400.

4. Bodde, *China's First Unifier*, p. 150. Note that a prime factor in the success of the unification of the script was the destruction of so many old books, a fact which has led many to believe that the Burning of the Books may have been a spin-off of Li Si's script unification scheme, and not necessarily anything to do with the suppression of unwelcome ideas. There are obvious parallels with the simplification of Chinese in the People's Republic in the 1950s, an effort that, even assuming it had been well intentioned, also served to render many pre-Revolution texts impenetrable to graduates of the modern educational system. Although the simplified script is supposed to make life easier, it is little help to the Sinologist, who must learn the unsimplified forms anyway if he wishes to read anything written before the 1950s, or indeed anything published in non-Communist China (Taiwan).

5. Bodde, *China's First Unifier*, p. 179.

6. See Wise, *Rattling the Cage*, p. 27.

7. Qin was not the only state in China to do this. During the later Han dynasty, Sima Qian himself, the author of the *Record of the Historian*, suffered a sentence of castration, but was only forced to undergo the punishment when he missed a payment on his opt-out fine.

8. *GSR*, I: 333.

9. Loewe, *Biographical Dictionary*, pp. 437–9, 705.

10. Hulsewé, *Remnants of Ch'in Law*, p. 184.

11. *Ibid.*, p. 187 (E6).

12. *Ibid.*, p. 202 (E22).

13. *Ibid.*, pp. 189–92.

14. *Ibid.*, pp. 194–5 (E16).

15. *Ibid.*, p. 102. Rank, however, was not a transferable commodity. If an individual was promoted for military service but died before the promotion could be carried out, his successor would not inherit the rank. *Ibid.*, p. 82 (A90).

16. *Ibid.*, p. 198 (E20).

17. *Ibid.*, p. 200 (E21).

18. *Ibid.*, p. 121 (D2).

19. *Ibid.*, p. 123 (D11).

20. *Ibid.*, pp. 124–5, (D13–15).
21. *Ibid.*, p. 137 (D48).
22. *Ibid.*, p. 137.
23. *Ibid.*, p. 123 (D10).
24. *Ibid.*, pp. 102–3. We do not know the precise level of accuracy required, but in the following Han dynasty, six out of every twelve arrows/quarrels were expected to hit a target. Each successful hit above the minimum six would win a marksman two weeks' bonus, up to a presumed maximum of three months, either in pay or time off in lieu.
25. *Ibid.*, p. 135 (D45).
26. *Ibid.*, pp. 127–8 (D21–3). It is interesting to note that there is such a thing as a 'botched' sacrifice. Presumably, these are ones where the omens do not live up to priests' expectations.
27. *Ibid.*, p. 83 (A83). Compare this attitude with that of Confucius, who famously showed great compassion for the disabled: see Clements, *Confucius*, p. 121.

Chapter Five

1. Barnes, *Rise of Civilization*, p. 169.
2. Hung, 'Ch'in Shi Huang', p. 13.
3. 'Great Wall of China', *Encyclopaedia Britannica*, 5: 449.
4. Di Cosmo, *Ancient China and its Enemies*, p. 140.
5. Hulsewé, *Remnants of Ch'in Law*, pp. 33, 71 (A69). Hulsewé takes particular interest in the size of wall-builder rations, since he was himself once an inmate in a Japanese prison camp. He notes that wall-builders, if fed according to the rules, were significantly better provisioned than Japanese POWs.
6. Geil, *Great Wall of China*, p. 104.
7. *Ibid.*, pp. 101, 106; Shao, 'What Is the Origin . . . ?', p. 163.
8. Geil, *Great Wall of China*, pp. 103–6.
9. Reuters, 'Rice a Building Block in China', 1 March 2005.
10. Geil, *Great Wall of China*, p. 63.
11. *Ibid.*, p. 106.
12. GSR, I: 138; Momiyama, *Shin no Shikôtei*, pp. 138–41.

Chapter Six

1. Yoshikawa, *Shin no Shikôtei*, p. 168. Yoshikawa's source is *Feng's Miscellany* (*Feng-shi Tingjian Ji*, or *Mr Feng's Record of Things Heard and Seen*), a Tang dynasty compilation by Feng Yuan. The journey to Mount Yi is recorded, sans folklore, in *GSR*, I: 138.
2. Yuan and Xiao, *Tales of Emperor Qin Shihuang*, pp. 92–3; *GSR*, I: 138.
3. *SJ*, p. 340; final two sentences from *GSR*, I: 139.
4. Yuan and Xiao, *Tales of Emperor Qin Shihuang*, pp. 97–8.
5. *GSR*, I: 142.
6. *SJ*, p. 344; *GSR*, I: 142.
7. *GSR*, I: 142.
8. Yoshikawa, *Shin no Shikôtei*, pp. 176–7, quoting *Shui Jing Zhu* (*Commentary on the River Classic*), by Li Daoyuan. A depiction of the workmen tumbling over as a dragon snaps their rope is included in the carvings of the Wuliang shrine, implying that although recorded in the northern Wei, the folktale of the search for the Ninth Tripod dates back at least as far as the Han dynasty, if not to the time of the First Emperor himself.
9. *GSR*, I: 142; Yuan and Xiao, *Tales of Emperor Qin Shihuang*, pp. 102–3.
10. Yuan and Xiao, *Tales of Emperor Qin Shihuang*, p. 111; *GSR*, I: 143.
11. *GSR*, I: 143; Loewe, *Biographical Dictionary*, pp. 683–4; Yuan and Xiao, *Tales of Emperor Qin Shihuang*, pp. 113–14. Zhang Liang would eventually come out of hiding during the unrest that followed the First Emperor's death, when he played a leading role in the foundation of the Han dynasty. Loewe, *Biographical Dictionary*, p. 19, suggests that Cang Hai may have been the name of a group of disaffected people and not a single individual.
12. *GSR*, I: 144.
13. Clements, *Confucius*, p. 68.
14. *GSR*, I: 144. See also *GSR*, I: 149, which implies that hallucinogens were among the many immortality recipes the

emperor tried. If he spent part of the time suffering the after-effects of supposed immortality 'drugs', then some of his later irrational behaviour makes more sense.

15. Yuan and Xiao, *Tales of Emperor Qin Shihuang*, p. 106.
16. *Ibid.*, p. 129. The jester You Zhan's comedic attitude won him a lot of friends in the palace, particularly among the palace guards, whom he once summoned in the middle of a banquet, thereby revealing to the emperor that they had been standing watch outside in the rain. He would even survive the Second Emperor, lampooning Huhai's plans to paint Xianyang's city walls by asking where a large enough room could be found to leave the city to dry in.
17. Later walls, most famously that of the Ming dynasty, would return to the Shanhai Pass as a borderline between civilised south and barbarian north. See Clements, *Pirate King*, pp. 85–8.
18. *GSR*, I: 145–6.
19. *GSR*, I: 147.
20. *GSR*, I: 150.
21. *GSR*, I: 150n., disputes the nature of live burial, and suggests that the First Emperor invited them to observe the bizarre phenomenon of melons that had bloomed in winter, but had previously ordered pitfall traps to be dug beneath them. However, it would have to be a large and complex pit-trap indeed that could ensnare 460 scholars at once.
22. Knoblock and Riegel, *Annals of Lü Buwei*, pp. 165–6.
23. *GSR*, I: 151; Yuan and Xiao, *Tales of Emperor Qin Shihuang*, p. 107.

Chapter Seven

1. Loewe, *Biographical Dictionary*, p. 652.
2. *GSR*, VII: 342.
3. *GSR*, VII: 343.
4. Although there is no mention of it in the *Record of the Historian*, later fictional sources often imply that Fusu was Li Si's son-in-law. If true, it shines new light on Li Si's attempt

to remove all other princes from the succession during the First Emperor's lifetime, and adds a new twist to their falling out over the Burning of the Books. Li Si might have initially promoted Fusu as a controllable candidate for Second Emperor, only to realise his error when Fusu stood up to him. Perhaps this is another reason why Li Si's decision to betray Fusu is so loaded with tension in contemporary accounts. If Li Si's daughter was still alive, he would be betraying her at the same time. If he had a grandson through Fusu, perhaps one he had hoped to install one day as a filial Third Emperor, then he was also signing the boy's death warrant.

5. Loewe, *Biographical Dictionary*, p. 229, suggests Li Si was more active in the deception. *GSR*, VII: 341, also implies that Li Si had a premonition of the coming danger at a banquet a year or so earlier, although his complaints that things could only get worse could have just as easily been a backhanded boast that he could not imagine how things could get better.

6. *GSR*, VII: 346, has twelve brothers killed in the capital and ten sisters dismembered at a place called Du; *GSR*, I: 157, mentions six dead in Du, implying the victims are all male (although presumably their spouses suffered similar fates, and may have been the 'princesses'), and a further three brothers forced to commit suicide in the capital. It is a mystery why the Historian contradicts himself. An 'inner palace' arrest suggests that the last three princes were quite young, perhaps even children, hence my use of the term 'boys'. Archaeologists at the Mount Li site have found seven graves, which are presumed to be those of the First Emperor's sons, but more may await discovery; 'Ch'in Tomb', *Encyclopaedia Britannica*, 3: 220.

7. Zhang, *The Qin Terracotta Army*, p. 77.

8. *GSR*, I: 148. Apang (also O-p'ang, Epang) seems to have referred to the 'hipped' tetrahedral roof planned for the palace. 'At its completion,' suggests the *Record of the Historian*, 'he would have selected a better name to call it.'

9. *GSR*, I: 157.

192

10. Hulsewé, *Remnants of Qin Law*, pp. 102–3.
11. Loewe, *Biographical Dictionary*, p. 38.
12. *GSR*, I: 159.
13. *GSR*, VII: 159–60; I: 347, 351–2.
14. *GSR*, VII: 354.
15. *GSR*, VII: 356; I: 161. The two accounts in the *Record of the Historian* differ slightly in chronology and motivation, but I have combined them here.
16. *GSR*, I: 162.
17. *GSR*, VII: 356.

Epilogue

1. Mao, *Discovery of the Eighth Wonder*, p. 19. Mount Li was also a site sacred to Nüwa, the ancient goddess who had repaired the 'hole in the sky' in the time of legends. According to a local folktale, a statue of Nüwa had come alive in the presence of the First Emperor while he was fantasising about sex with her. The statue spat in the emperor's face, causing a malignant growth to form. After a prolonged penance lasting forty-nine days, the First Emperor was granted a reprieve, and the affliction was removed by bathing in the hot springs that sprang up on the mountainside. Yuan and Xiao, *Tales of Emperor Qin Shihuang*, p. 156.
2. *Ibid.*, pp. 37–8.
3. *Ibid.*, p. 42.
4. Zhang, *The Qin Terracotta Army*, pp. 31–2.
5. *Ibid.*, pp. 41–2.
6. *Ibid.*, p. 45.
7. *Ibid.*, p. 62.
8. *Ibid.*, p. 17.
9. *GSR*, I: 155.

Sources and Further Reading

Barnes, G., *The Rise of Civilization in East Asia: The Archaeology of China, Korea and Japan*, London, Thames & Hudson, 1999

Bauer, W. and Herbert Franke, *The Golden Casket: Chinese Novellas of Two Millennia*, trans. Christopher Levenson, Harmondsworth, Penguin, 1967

Birrell, A., *Chinese Mythology: An Introduction*, Baltimore, John Hopkins University Press, 1993

Bodde, D., *China's First Unifier*, Leiden, E.J. Brill, 1967

——, 'The State and Empire of Ch'in', in D. Twitchett and M. Loewe (eds), *The Cambridge History of China*, Cambridge, Cambridge University Press, 1986, vol. 1, pp. 21–102

Chang, K., *Art, Myth, and Ritual: The Path to Political Authority in Ancient China*, Cambridge, MA, Harvard University Press, 1983

Clements, J., *Confucius: A Biography*, Stroud, Sutton Publishing, 2004

——, *Pirate King: Coxinga and the Fall of the Ming Dynasty*, Stroud, Sutton Publishing, 2004

Cotterell, A., *The First Emperor of China*, London, Macmillan, 1981

Cottrell, L., *The Tiger of Ch'in: How China Became a Nation*, London, Evans Brothers, 1962

Crump, J., *Chan-kuo Ts'e*, Ann Arbor, Center for Chinese Studies, University of Michigan, 1996

Di Cosmo, N., *Ancient China and Its Enemies: The Rise of Nomadic Power in East Asian History*, Cambridge, Cambridge University Press, 2002

Fryer, J., *The Great Wall of China*, London, New English Library, 1977

Fu, Z., *China's Legalists: The Earliest Totalitarians and Their Art of Ruling*, Armonk, NY, M.E. Sharpe, 1996

Geil, W., *The Great Wall of China*, London, John Murray, 1909

Harper, D., 'Warring States, Qin, and Han Manuscripts Related to Natural Philosophy and the Occult', in Edward Shaughnessy (ed.), *New Sources of Early Chinese History: An Introduction to the Reading of Inscriptions and Manuscripts*, Berkeley, Society for the Study of Early China and the Institute of East Asian Studies, 1997, pp. 223–52

Hulsewé, A. (ed.), *Remnants of Ch'in Law: An Annotated Translation of the Ch'in Legal and Administrative Rules of the 3rd Century B.C. Discovered in Yün-meng Prefecture, Hu-pei Province, in 1975*, Leiden, E.J. Brill, 1985

Hung, S., 'The Age in which Ch'in Shi Huang Was Born', in Y. Li (ed.), *The First Emperor of China*, White Plains, NY, International Arts and Sciences Press, 1975, pp. 3–16

——, 'The Establishment of a New System for the Consolidation of Unification', in Li, *First Emperor of China*, pp. 91–115

——, 'The Preparations for Unification', in Li, *First Emperor of China*, pp. 37–54

——, 'The Success of Unification', in Li, *First Emperor of China*, pp. 74–90

Knoblock, J., *Xunzi: A Translation and Study of the Complete Works*, 3 vols, Stanford, CT, Stanford University Press, 1988, 1990, 1994

—— and Jeffrey Riegel (eds), *The Annals of Lü Buwei: A Complete Translation and Study*, Stanford, CT, Stanford University Press, 2000

Kronk, G., *Cometography: A Catalog of Comets*, vol. 1, *Ancient–1799*, Cambridge, Cambridge University Press, 1999

Landers, J., 'The Political Thought of Han Fei', PhD thesis, Indiana University, 1972

Li, Y. (ed.), *The First Emperor of China*, White Plains, NY, International Arts and Sciences Press, 1975

Lo, S., 'The Struggle between Restoration and Counter-Restoration in the Course of the Founding of the Ch'in Dynasty', in Y. Li (ed.), *The First Emperor of China*, White Plains, NY, International Arts and Sciences Press, 1975, pp. 55–73

Loewe, M., *A Biographical Dictionary of the Qin, Former Han and Xin Periods (221 BC–AD 24)*, Leiden, E.J. Brill, 2000

Mao, Q., *The Discovery of the Eighth Wonder of the World*, trans. Zhou Longru, Xi'an, Shaanxi People's Art Publishing House, 1985

Momiyama, A., *Shin no Shikôtei [Qin Shihuangdi]*, Tokyo, Hakutaisha, 1994

Nienhauser, W. (ed.), *The Grand Scribe's Records*, vol. I, *The Basic Annals of Pre-Han China*, Bloomington, IN, Indiana University Press, 1994

——, *The Grand Scribe's Records*, vol. VII, *The Memoirs of Pre-Han China*, Bloomington, IN, Indiana University Press, 1994

Ramsey, S., *The Languages of China*, Princeton, NJ, Princeton University Press, 1987

Reuters, 'Rice a Building Block in China', 1 March 2005

Sage, S., *Ancient Sichuan and the Unification of China*, Albany, State University of New York Press, 1992

Shao, H., 'What Is the Origin of "the Wailing of Meng Chiang-nü at the Great Wall"?', in Y. Li (ed.), *The First Emperor of China*, White Plains, NY, International Arts and Sciences Press, 1975, pp. 162–3

Tinios, E. (ed.), *Emperors, Barbarians and Historians in Early Imperial China*, Leeds, School of History, University of Leeds, 1995

—— (ed.), *Han Shu 94: Memoir on the Hsiung-nu*, Leeds, School of History, University of Leeds, 1995

Wagner, D., *Iron and Steel in Ancient China*, Leiden, E.J. Brill, 1993

Wang, H. and Leo S. Chang, *The Philosophical Foundations of Han Fei's Political Theory*, Monographs of the Society for Asian and Comparative Philosophy, no. 7, Honolulu, University of Hawaii Press, 1986

Watson, B. (ed.), *Records of the Grand Historian: Qin Dynasty*, Hong Kong, Columbia University Press, 1993

Wei, C., 'Ch'in Shih-huang's Book-burning as Seen from the Bamboo Slips Unearthed in Ying-ch'üeh-shan', in Y. Li (ed.), *The First Emperor of China*, White Plains, NY, International Arts and Sciences Press, 1975, pp. 145–53

Wirgin, J., *The Emperor's Warriors: Catalogue of the Exhibition of the Terracotta Figures of Warriors and Horses of the Qin Dynasty of China*, trans. A.S. Winstanley, Edinburgh, City of Edinburgh Museums and Art Galleries, 1985

Wise, S., *Rattling the Cage: Towards Legal Rights for Animals*, Cambridge, MA, Perseus Books, 2000

Yao, X., *An Introduction to Confucianism*, Cambridge, Cambridge University Press, 2000

Yoshikawa, T., *Shin no Shikôtei [Qin Shihuangdi]*, Tokyo, Kodansha, 2002

Yuan, K., *Dragons and Dynasties: An Introduction to Chinese Mythology*, Harmondsworth, Penguin, 1991

Yuan, Y. and Xiao Ding, *Tales of Emperor Qin Shihuang*, Beijing, Foreign Languages Press, 1999

Zhang, W., *The Qin Terracotta Army: Treasures of Lintong*, London, Scala Books and Cultural Relics Publishing House, 1996

Index

Index

Yan, *see* Land of Swallows

Yang Peiyan 155

Yang Wenxue 155

Yaojia 72–3

Yellow River 18, 77, 79, 87, 104, 136

Yellow Sovereign 16, 19

Ying Xiong 180

Ying Zheng 1, 8, 41, 48–9, 66, 68, 90, 131; ancestors of 18–22, 36, 184; education of 43–6; assassination attempts on 11, 56, 78, 91, 121, 124, 182; name of 18, 35, 82–3, 184; palace of 9; succession crisis 53–5, 84; and Red Prince 1–9, 74–7, 82; superstition of 66, 114–5, 108, 117–8, 120–1, 132–3, 135, 193; proclamations of 57, 69, 78–9, 81–2, 115, 118–9, 137, 138; fictional accounts of 76, 106–9, 124, 177–80; travels of 110, 113–23, 125–6, 136–8; tomb of 162–7

Yiren 31, 34–8, 41–2, 50–1

You Zhan 125, 191

Yue barbarians (Viet) 127

Yueyang, 178

Zao Fu 19, 184

Zhang Fengyi 179

Zhang Han 147–8, 150, 154, 159, 162

Zhang Liang 122, 190

Zhao Gao 60, 86, 91–2, 121–2, 136, 138, 139–45, 148–54, 166, 184

Zhao Sheng 184

Zhao, *see* Land of Latecoming

Zhaocheng 184

Zhaoji 35, 37, 41–2, 48, 50–1, 58, 137, 177, 185, as regent: 42–3, 54–5, implication in attempted coup 51–7

Zheng Canal 49, 59, 71

Zheng Zhenduo 162

Zhong Fu, *see* Lü Buwei

Zhou dynasty 17, 19, 20, 21, 22, 25, 26, 29, 38–9, 40, 41–3, 63, 65, 79, 82, 84, 85, 86, 99, 119

Ziying, *see* Prince/King Ziying